CW00825617

IN THE LIKENESS OF SINFUL FLESH

IN THE LIKENESS OF SINFUL FLESH

An Essay on the Humanity of Christ

by

Thomas Weinandy, O.F.M. CAP.

T&T CLARK
EDINBURGH

T&T CLARK
59 GEORGE STREET
EDINBURGH EH2 2LQ
SCOTLAND

First published 1993

ISBN 0 567 09643 2

British Library Cataloguing-in-Publication Data
A catalogue record for this book
is available from the British Library

Typeset by Trinity Typesetting, Edinburgh
Printed and bound in Great Britain by Bookcraft, Avon

To Jesus the Lord and King,
In Whom Alone We Have Salvation

CONTENTS

FOREWORD

Earlier this century, George Tyrrell famously commented that the modern movement to recover the humanity of Jesus through historical-critical research had produced merely an idealized portrait of itself. The process has scarcely slackened since his time. Jesus the bourgeois moralist and Jesus the progressive liberator are one at least in this, that their begetters tend to know better who Jesus really is than the New Testament texts, which are still suspected of losing the real Jesus beneath the encrustations of dogma. Breaking into that world of competing liberalisms, Dr Weinandy proposes to show that a truly human Christ is not to be found by rejecting the dogmatic tradition, but by faithful exegesis of the biblical texts as they stand. His method is to bring to the light of day elements under-emphasized, but none the less truly present, in the Christian tradition.

What we find in this clear, interesting and lucid study is a dogmatic christology that does not play scripture and tradition — or the humanity and divinity of Christ — against one another, but brings them into positive engagement. The author's basic concern is to give due account of the saving humanity of Christ, and in this the notion that he bore our sinful humanity is central. It is not, of course, that Jesus sinned, but that the humanity he bore was like ours in being subject to the pressures and temptations that lead to sin in the rest of us fallen creatures. 'Ultimately, our salvation is unconditionally dependent upon the Son's assuming a humanity disfigured by sin and freely acting as a son of Adam.'

Dr Weinandy's theme is advanced first by a historical study of the tradition. There is encouragement to be found in a minority of the Fathers, in Anselm — though his vision is flawed — and in Aquinas, unexpectedly for those who know only that of his christology which suggests the opposite. After appeal to some recent Reformed christology, the bulk of the book is then devoted to the biblical treatment of the humanity of Jesus, and attention is properly given to such crucial episodes as the baptism and temptations, as well as to the traditionally dogmatic themes of christology.

A theologian of the Reformed tradition might well want to put some of this rather differently, and while welcoming the use made of the theology of the great Edward Irving — surely a modern pioneer of this approach — I would also point to its anticipation in the thought of the Puritan, John Owen, as Alan Spence's research, some of it published, has shown. What is particularly important about Owen is that his work was written in disagreement with the Socinians, whose typically modernist approach to christology at once rules out a positive evaluation of the orthodox tradition and is so influential in the modern world. (Correspondingly, I would be less inclined to call Karl Barth in evidence, chiefly for the reason that his uncompromising concentration on divine action in Christ leaves little room for more than the bare assertion of Jesus' sinful humanity.)

But the sharpest questions must come at a point of which nothing is made by the author. Can all that Dr Weinandy wants to say be upheld while the teaching of the immaculate conception continues to be official Catholic doctrine? I would not want to tempt Dr Weinandy into indiscretion here, but to suggest that the logic of his writing will inevitably cause questions of this kind to be asked. It is, in my opinion, a far

stronger reason for not becoming a Catholic than the analogy
of being (which remains a barrier, despite the widespread
misunderstanding of the point of Barth's polemic against it).

But I must end, as I began, with a wholly positive judge-
ment. There appear at present to be two points of convergence
between the Roman Catholic and Protestant Traditions, and
they are far apart from one another. One is where some streams
of Catholic thought are converging with nineteenth century
Protestant modernism. The other is to be found in approaches
which reach deeper into the historic and orthodox Christian
traditions in order to find and develop the dogmatic basis for
a new and truly theological convergence. Dr Weinandy belongs firmly in the latter movement, and that is why, in the
opinion of one Protestant at least, his study is to be warmly
welcomed.

Colin Gunton
King's College, London
1 May 1992

PREFACE

This essay studies the humanity of Jesus, specifically, that in the Incarnation, the eternal Son of God assumed not some ideal humanity, but our sinful humanity. This is a soteriological essay in that it seeks to demonstrate that only in assuming a humanity of the fallen race of Adam, and living and dying within such a humanity, did the Son redeem us and make us new. Jesus' bearing the birthmark of sin is the foundation for any authentic understanding of the Incarnation and the work of redemption.

This essay has a rather lengthy evolution, one that has intimately involved my own theological and spiritual journey. Since my student days, both in the seminary and as a doctoral candidate, I have had a great interest in the Incarnation. During these years, I came to appreciate and reverence the truth that Jesus is truly the Son of God incarnate. My understanding of Jesus' full divinity and his authentic humanity grew and deepened.

Nonetheless, fourteen years ago, I could not have written this essay. In the ensuring years, two factors have formed and molded me. Initially my Christology, while consistent with the basic New Testament proclamation, was primarily historical and doctrinal. The Fathers of the Church and the early Councils plus the philosophical insights of systematic theology fashioned my thought. I lacked a thoroughly biblical Christology, one that would enhance and enliven this doctrinal foundation. Over the intervening years, I have come to love the scriptural proclamation of Jesus. Through prayerfully reading and studying the Scriptures, I have come to learn and articulate what I have now written. The Bible is the fundamental source of this essay.

Secondly and concurrently, the teaching of the Mother of God Community, of which I have been a member for sixteen years, was the impetus and inspiration both for delving more deeply into the Scriptures and for perceiving, to an even greater extent, the significance of the Incarnation and the marvellous work of redemption. Specifically, the Spirit's teaching this Community the significance of the cross of Jesus Christ has nurtured this present work. We have learned in a fresh and experiential manner that on the cross Jesus put our sinful flesh to death and we are now empowered to live a radically new life in the Holy Spirit. The blood of Jesus has cleansed us of sin, reconciled us to the Father, and so made us new creations in Christ.

The appropriation of this Gospel truth has not only changed my life, but also the lives of many others. This experience compelled me to re-examine and re-think my Christology and soteriology. This essay is the fruit of this re-examination.

Thus, this essay is born of Scripture, the teaching of the Mother of God Community, and the Community's lived experience. This essay, although in many ways academic, is founded upon not merely the learned insights of theology, but also upon the daily life of a body of Christian men and women. Hopefully, this gives to my study a living link to the scriptural proclamation, to the apostolic community, and to the heritage of the Church's saints. This, after all, is the true meaning of the Church's understanding of tradition — the living and ever-growing inheritance of the past brought to life in the present faithful. Similarly, I hope that this essay then bears the imprint not of a lifeless and sterile treatise, but of the Holy Spirit who makes ever new the work of Christ in God's people.

I want to thank Frs Gerard Beigel, Michael Duggan, Peter Hocken, Francis Martin, and Theophane Rush for their encouragement and for sharing with me their theological and scriptural expertise. I also want to thank Laura Millman for her editorial assistance. Lastly, I am grateful to my Capuchin brothers for their generous and continued support of my pastoral and academic endeavours.

Feast of St Bernard of Clairvaux, 1992.

PART ONE:

A CONTEMPORARY WORK OF THE SPIRIT

In all ages, the Holy Spirit engenders faith in Jesus Christ (see Jn 14:26; 1 Cor 12:3). Thankfully, our age is not exempt. Because we wish to build upon this contemporary grace, we will first examine some aspects of today's Christology to discern what is truly of the Spirit before we enter into the heart of our essay. This brief inquiry will also allow us to place our study within the present christological setting.

CHAPTER ONE

THE RE-EMERGENCE OF THE HUMAN JESUS

Contemporary Christology exhibits a keen theological and historical interest in the human Jesus.[1] This is so for a variety of reasons which we describe below.

No More Docetism!

Firstly, many theologians continue to react to a theological past that they interpret as having overemphasized the divinity of Jesus to the detriment of his humanity. Manual Christology in the 19th and early 20th centuries, in defending the faith against the Enlightenment and Modernism, concentrated on apologetics, endeavoring to prove Jesus' divinity principally through his miracles and Johannine theology. The inherited scholastic tradition, in light of this emphasis on the divine, portrayed Jesus as exhibiting little, if any, frailty and ignorance.[2] Many contemporary theologians argue that such stress on Jesus' divine personhood and his human perfection casts a

---

[1] See, e.g., Monika Hellwig's excellent summary of recent Christology: "Re-Emergence of the Human, Critical, Public Jesus," *Theological Studies* 50 (1989) 466-80. See also Elizabeth Johnson, *Consider Jesus: Waves of Renewal in Christology* (New York: Crossroad, 1990), 19-65. Also William M. Thompson, *The Jesus Debate: A Survey and Synthesis* (New York: Paulist Press, 1985), 14-78.

[2] See, e.g., J.M. Herve, *Manuale Theologiae Dogmaticae,* Vol. 2 (Paris: Apud Berche et Pagis, 1959), 456-67.

docetic or monophysite hue upon Christology, at least on the popular, devotional level.[3] Thus reverberating within many recent books and articles is the cry—"No more Docetism!"[4] Numerous recent theologians underscore the Church's tradition and the Council of Chalcedon's demand that Jesus was fully man, *homoousios* (of the same nature) with us in every way.

Secondly, contemporary theologians have a renewed appreciation that Jesus lived within and was molded by a genuine historical and cultural milieu. What he said and did as a human being are the making of history and not divine theatrics done within some platonic, ahistorical vacuum. Thus, scriptural studies today feature Jesus' historical setting and his Jewish cultural conditioning within contemporary Palestinian

---

[3] While granting the legitimate concern over docetic Christology on the popular level in the past, we suggest that this fear should not be exaggerated. Within the Church, there was also an authentic devotion to the humanity of Christ. The popular devotion to the Sacred Heart of Jesus testifies to this. This devotion kept alive an appropriate understanding of the Incarnation and of the humanity of Jesus. Cf. Pope Pius XII, *Haurietis Aquas (On Devotion to the Sacred Heart)*, 1956; Karl Rahner, "Devotion to the Sacred Heart," *Theological Investigations,* Vol. 3, Part Five (Baltimore: Helicon Press, 1967), 321-52. See also, Annice Callahan, *Karl Rahner's Spirituality of the Pierced Heart: A Reinterpretation of Devotion to the Sacred Heart* (Washington, DC: University Press of America, 1990).

[4] Cf. John Hick, ed., *The Myth of God Incarnate* (London: SCM, 1977); John Knox, *The Humanity and Divinity of Christ* (Cambridge: University Press, 1967); John Macquarrie, *Jesus Christ in Modern Thought* (London\Philadelphia: SCM\Trinity Press International, 1990); Gerald O'Collins, *What Are They Saying About Jesus?* (New York: Paulist Press, 1977); Norman Pittenger, *Christology Reconsidered* (London: SCM Press, 1970); J.A.T. Robinson, *The Human Face of God* (London: SCM, 1973); Karl Rahner, "Current Problems in Christology," *Theological Investigations,* Vol. I (Baltimore: Helicon Press, 1961), 149-200; Thompson, 45-49.

Judaism.[5] A better understanding of first-century Judaism plus the mining of the Synoptic tradition has contributed greatly to this new awareness.

Thirdly, the motivation propelling these new emphases is the realization that if Jesus is to be credible to contemporary men and women, he must be like us. This is rightly a soteriological emphasis. Jesus must not remain an isolated stranger to our personal struggles and to our universal needs. He must have been truly tempted; experienced hunger and thirst, alienation and hardship; suffered persecution and injustice; and finally have died as an outcast. Thus systematic theologians and Scripture scholars, working from within a Christology "from below," probe his human consciousness and knowledge searching for the basis of his filial relationship to his Father, his self-understanding, and his awareness of his mission.[6] Moreover, Jesus' personality—his kindness, mercy, moral integrity, intolerance of injustice, and love for the

---

[5] Cf. R.E. Brown, "Who Do Men Say That I Am?—A Survey of Modern Scholarship on Gospel Christology," *Biblical Reflections on Crises Facing the Church* (New York: Paulist Press, 1975), 20-37; O. Cullmann, *The Christology of the New Testament* (Philadelphia: Westminster Press, 1959); R.H. Fuller, *The Foundations of New Testament Christology* (London: Collins, 1965); R. Fuller and P. Perkins, *Who Is This Christ?* (Philadelphia: Westminster Press, 1983); E.P. Sanders, *Jesus and Judaism* (Philadelphia: Fortress, 1985); Donald Senior, *Jesus, A Gospel Portrait* (Dayton: Pflaum Press, 1975); Gerard Sloyan, *Jesus in Focus: A Life in Its Setting* (Mystic, CT: Twenty-Third Publications, 1983); Anthony Tambasco, *In the Days of Jesus: The Jewish Background and Unique Teaching of Jesus* (New York: Paulist, 1983); Geza Vermes, *Jesus the Jew* (Philadelphia: Fortress, 1981). See also, Hellwig, 470-71; Johnson, 49-65, Thompson, 151-80.

[6] This is admirably exemplified in the studies done on Jesus' use of the word "Abba" in addressing and praying to his Father. Cf. J. Jeremias, "Abba" in *The Prayers of Jesus* (STB II 6) (London: 1967), 11-65; and his *New Testament Theology*, I (London: SCM Press, 1972), 61-67.

poor—forms the basis of today's apostolically oriented spirituality with its emphasis on praxis.[7]

Thus, contemporary Christology confirms the importance
of the historical Jesus. No longer are Christians satisfied solely
with the so-called Christ of faith. The Christ in whom we
believe must be in continuity with the Jesus of history.[8]

Undoubtedly, this contemporary interest in the humanity
of Jesus has great merit. The sincere desire to be in touch with
the authentic Jesus and not with some theological fabrication
divorced from real life testifies to the Spirit's work in our day.
However, without denying the absolute legitimacy of the
emphasis on the historical Jesus with its accompanying scriptural and systematic developments, we suggest that some
aspects of contemporary Christology are deficient. As we will
explain, the deficiency ironically bears directly upon the
Spirit's contemporary movement, i.e., treasuring Jesus' humanity and his human historical words and deeds.

The reason the Spirit desires to lead us even more deeply
today into the humanity of Jesus is that only within his
humanity do we find the love of the Father and our eternal
salvation. The humanity of Jesus is the foundation of the
Church, and the source of our prayer and sacramental worship.
Today's authentic movements of renewal within all Christian
bodies testify, as did all those of the past, that *Jesus* alone is
Lord.

[7] Liberation theology is a primary example of this emphasis. See also,
Monika Hellwig, *Jesus, the Compassion of God* (Wilmington, DE: Michael
Glazier, 1983). Also Thompson, 299-427.

[8] For studies which argue for the continuity between the Jesus of history
and the Christ of faith, cf. I.H. Marshall, *I Believe in the Historical Jesus*
(Grand Rapids: Eerdmans, 1977); I.H. Marshall, *The Origins of New
Testament Christology* (Downers Grove, IL: InterVarsity, 1976); C.F.D.
Moule, The *Origin of Christology* (Cambridge: University Press, 1977);
Gerald O'Collins, *Interpreting Jesus* (New York: Paulist Press, 1983), 35-72.

In this chapter, we will briefly touch upon a few, critical misconceptions prevalent in some of today's Christology. Then, we will address at length the subject of how a fuller understanding of Jesus' humanity contributes to a more accurate and complete soteriology. In so doing, we wish to address the genuine concerns of the authentic developments within contemporary Christology and so enhance its strengths.

Divinity Vs. Humanity

We need to address two misconceptions concerning Jesus' humanity. The first focuses on the nature of the Incarnation. The prevailing thought asserts that advocating the utterly divine personhood of Jesus, as the Council of Chalcedon defined it and tradition has understood and affirmed it, is to subvert the reality of his complete humanity. Simply put, if Jesus is a divine person, he cannot be a human person. Thus, this thinking deprives him of something absolutely essential to authentic humanness—the integrity of his own distinctive and integral human personality.[9]

However, to uphold the complete humanity of Christ at the slightest expense to his divinity is to sabotage the very reason for Jesus' being fully human. In the Incarnation, the Church proclaims the complete divinity and humanity of Christ not for their own sake, but for the sake of the other. The Incarnation demands that God truly *is* man, that it is truly *God* who is man, and that it is truly *man* that God is.[10] Thus, if it is not

---

[9] For examples of this concern, see references cited in footnote 4. For a good survey and expression of this contemporary concern see Thompson, 299-311, 330-33, 367-72, 386-94. For an excellent critique see Richard Sturch, *The Word and the Christ* (Oxford: Clarendon Press, 1991).

[10] See Thomas Aquinas, *Summa Theologica*, III,16,1, trs. Dominican Fathers (New York: Benzinger Brothers, 1947). See also, Thomas Weinandy, *Does God Change? The Word's Becoming in the Incarnation* (Petersham, MA: St. Bede's, 1985), 82.

the Son of God in the fullness of his divinity who is fully and completely man, then the whole point of Jesus' being totally human is lost. Paradoxically, to preserve the complete humanity of Jesus while sacrificing his divine personhood is to depreciate radically the relevance of the humanity. (The reverse is equally true. To uphold the divine personhood of Jesus at the sacrifice of his humanity would make his divinity irrelevant.) The significance of the historical, tangible, Jewish man Jesus is precisely that he who is this man is none other than the Son. If we do not hear, see, feel, and touch the divine Son in and through his human words and historical actions, then what we hear and see will only be, at best, supplementary to and of a piece with other exceptional moral leaders or religious philosophers. Jesus' singular and irreducible uniqueness would disappear.

No More Kenoticism!

Thus, we must reject all classical and contemporary forms of kenotic Christology, even in their most discreet and delicate expressions.[11] Kenotic Christologies propose that the Son must either empty himself of—that is, give up—those divine

[11] For examples and studies of classical and contemporary kenotic Christology, see: Russell F. Aldwinckle, *More Than Man: A Study in Christology* (Grand Rapids: Eerdmans, 1976); Ray S. Anderson, *Historical Transcendence and the Reality of God: A Christological Critique* (London: Geoffrey Chapman, 1976); A.B. Bruce, *The Humiliation of Christ* (Edinburgh: T.& T. Clark, 1881); Charles Gore, *The Incarnation of the Son of God: The Bampton Lectures 1891* (London: John Murray, 1898); Francis J. Hall, *The Kenotic Theory* (New York: Longmans, Green and Co., 1898); P. Henry, "Kenose," *Dictionnaire de la Bible Supplement,* Vol. 5 (Paris: 1957), 7-162; John Stewart Lawton, *Conflict in Christology* (London: SPCK, 1947); Geddes MacGregor, *He Who Lets Us Be: A Theology of Love* (New York: Seabury, 1975); Thomas V. Morris, *The Logic of God Incarnate* (Ithaca: Cornell University Press, 1986); Lucien J. Richard, A *Kenotic Christology* (Washington, DC: University Press of America, 1982); William

attributes which are purportedly incompatible with the Incarnation (such as omniscience or omnipotence), or he must hold them in abeyance during his earthly human life. While it is inconceivable how God can give up or hold in check his omniscience or omnipotence, what is more to the point here is that even if he could do so, such an action would not facilitate but instead thoroughly corrupt a true understanding of the Incarnation.

Within his incarnate state, as he lives an authentic human life, the divine Son must be *homoousios* with the Father, in the fullness of his divine being. Otherwise, he is not truly God who is man but some lesser divine manifestation. There cannot be an *ad intra* or *in se* trinitarian expression of divine sonship differing from the *ad extra* or *pro me* expression of divine sonship as man. An authentic Incarnation insists they be identical.

Moreover, only if the Son of God was *homoousios* with the Father within his incarnate state (as man), could we come to know that the Son is *homoousios* with the Father within the Trinity. Only if the Son, in the fullness of his divinity, existed as man, and as man manifested the fullness of his divinity, could we come to know in faith that he is God as the Father is God. If the Son were incarnate in some lesser divine form, he could not reveal himself to be one in being with the Father, but could only display his inferior and reduced status.

The early christological councils were well aware of this. They defended the full divinity of Jesus not just for the sake of his being God (a trinitarian concern), but also for the sake of the Incarnation. The Nicene *homoousion* doctrine rose from, was defined within, and secured the truth of the Incarnation—

Thompson, *The Jesus Debate* (New York: Paulist Press, 1985); G. Wainwright, *Doxology* (New York: Oxford University Press, 1980); Frank Weston, *The One Christ* (London: Longmans, Green and Co., 1914).

who this man is ("who suffered under Pontius Pilate," etc.) must be the eternal Son of God. Otherwise, an authentic Incarnation had not taken place.[12]

Moreover, kenotic Christology not only calls into question Jesus' divinity, but also jeopardizes his full humanity. Kenotic Christologists "tone down" the divinity in order to make it compatible with the humanity, thus "giving up" or "holding in check" divine omniscience or omnipotence. However, the result is that Jesus then possessed, not a fully human consciousness, mind, and will, but a truncated or humanly equipped divine consciousness, mind, and will implanted in a humanoid. Kenotic Christology always gives birth to retarded Docetism or Monophysitism.

The primary misconception within kenotic Christology (which desires to maintain the divinity of the Son) and other Christologies (which would entirely sacrifice Jesus' divinity for the sake of his humanity) is that they conceive the classical interpretation of the Incarnation in an essentialist fashion. They envisage the act of incarnating as the bringing together and uniting of two contrary and incompatible natures or essences (divine and human) containing within themselves contradictory attributes (for example, omniscience and limited knowledge; omnipotence and limited power). Such an

---

[12] Following upon the *homoousios* doctrine of Nicea, both Nestorius and Cyril of Alexandria argued interestingly that the eternal Son must be immutable not only for the sake of his divinity (God cannot change), but also for the sake of his humanity. If the Son of God changed in becoming man, and thus lessened his divine status, then it is no longer truly God who is man. Cf. Weinandy, 32-66.

This point is obviously relevant for trinitarian thought as well. Only if the immanent Trinity revealed itself as it is in itself, within its economic trinitarian expression, could we come to know the trinity of persons as they actually exist. The *homoousion* doctrine guarantees that the economic Trinity is the immanent Trinity and vice versa.

essentialist understanding always leads, by necessity, to the Nestorian conundrum. Either the divinity or the humanity is necessarily jeopardized in the ontological union of natures or essences. Docetism and Monophysitism depreciate the humanity. Kenoticism undermines the full divinity. The only remaining option is to jettison this conception of the Incarnation outright and propose some form of adoptionism which is an appealing solution to many contemporary Christologists.

However, classical Christology, as the Council of Chalcedon defined it and such theologians as St. Cyril of Alexandria and St. Thomas Aquinas interpreted it, is not essentialistic, but personal/existential.[13] The Incarnation is not the fusing together of two incompatible natures (divine and human), but the person of the Son coming to exist as man or coming to be man. The union (the incarnating act) is personal (*hypostatic*) in that it is the bringing into existence a humanity and uniting it to the person of the Son, thus establishing the manner or mode of the Son's existence— as man. The incarnational becoming terminates in the person of the Son existing as a man. Obviously, the mystery still remains, but it endures in, hopefully, an intelligible and correctly conceived manner.

Even so, does not the divine person usurp the place of the human person thus rendering Jesus less than fully human? Kenoticists have taken this concern seriously and thoughtfully attempted to address it in an orthodox manner. However, building upon the personal/existential nature of the Incarnation, we assert that an insistence upon the divine personhood of Jesus in no way denies *any* aspect of his humanity.

---

[13] For the personal/existential understanding of the Incarnation in Cyril of Alexandria and Thomas Aquinas, see Weinandy, 46-66, 82-100. Within these pages, I develop further the ideas I express here concerning the whole personal/existential understanding of the Incarnation.

A Human "I"

If, as within the Trinity, we define "person" as a subsistent relation—an understanding forged within classical Augustinian and Thomistic Trinitarianism—we can also apply this concept to the Incarnation. Since the eternal Son is absolutely and purely relational in and of himself, he need never actualize any relational potential within himself in order to be related to something or someone else. Thus, he was (and is) able, within the Incarnation, to unite his humanity to himself as he is in himself (in the fullness of his divinity) to such a degree that he (the Son *homoousios* with the Father) related (and relates) to the world and other human beings as an authentic man. As incarnate, the Son possessed (and possesses) a human personality, a thoroughly human manner of relating.[14]

Jesus possessed not only a human body, mind, and will, but also a human center of self-consciousness, a human self-identity. He thought and spoke with the integrity of a thoroughly human "I". He was self-conscious, composed his thoughts, and spoke in an entirely human manner, with the human "I" of a man. When Jesus said, for example, "I have come not to abolish the Law and the prophets, but to fulfill them," (Mt 5:17), that "I" sprang from and manifested a human self-conscious awareness—a human "I". What the Incarnation demands is that he who embraced a human center

---

[14] For the development of the notion of "person" within trinitarian and christological thought, see J. O'Donnell, *The Mystery of the Triune God* (New York: Paulist Press, 1990), 100-111; G.L. Prestige, *God in Patristic Thought* (London: SPCK, 1952); Joseph Ratzinger, "Zum Personenverstandnis in der Theologie," *Dogma und Verkundigung* (Munich: Erich Wewel Verlag, 1973), 205-23, English tr., "Concerning the Notion of Person in Theology," *Communio* 17 (Fall, 1990): 439-54. For a contemporary understanding of "person" as relational, see Jean Galot, *The Person of Christ* (Chicago: Franciscan Herald Press, 1983); Weinandy, 88-100, 184-86.

of self-consciousness, and thought and spoke with an integral human "I," was the eternal Son. There was (and is) a human "I" of a divine person—of the Son. The identity of Jesus is the eternal Son. The mode of that identity is as a man. Properly understood then, we can truly say that the divine person of the Son (the who) spoke and acted as a human person (with a human "I").[15]

Within this understanding, Jesus lacks nothing that pertains to us as human beings. What is unique is that the divine person of the Son (the subject, the who) in the Incarnation lives, experiences himself, and expresses himself in a totally human manner, within the ambience of a human self-identity, under the conditions of a human "I".[16] Because the Son truly came to exist as man, he feels, thinks, speaks, and acts within the confines of a fully human "I."

Jesus as Unique

A second contemporary concern centers upon Jesus' definitive uniqueness as man. To sever the divinity of Jesus from his humanity devalues what he said and did as man. Often today, the primary hermeneutic for understanding Jesus' human words and deeds is that of archetype and model. We are to imitate his faithful obedience to the Father, his fortitude in suffering, his determination in the face of injustice, his selfless loyalty in the heat of temptation, and his kindness and gentleness in the midst of frustration and hopelessness. His presence and example as an archetype may act as the supreme

---

[15] Cf. J. Galot, *La Conscience de Jesus* (Gembloux: Duculot-Lethielleux, 1977); his *Who Is Christ?* (Chicago: Franciscan Herald Press, 1981), 319-39; also Sturch, *The Word and the Christ,* 121-41.

[16] See Bernard Lonergan, "Christ as Subject: A Reply," *Collection,* ed. Fredrick Crowe (New York: Herder and Herder, 1967), 164-97.

leaven in our lives and thus, within the march of history, yet it remains but one good example among others. Jesus, in all his humanness, remains but a source of encouragement, the personification of the universal moral imperative, of our own human spiritual and social self-development. But this interpretation diminishes Jesus. What Jesus did as a man does not bring about an effect in our relationship with God, with others, or within ourselves that differs in kind from the effects that any other good person achieved. Within this view, Jesus may have made the existing human condition better, but he did not substantially change or radically transform it.[17]

Christology From "Below" and "Above"

Finally within this context, we agree with most contemporary Christologists that all authentic Christology must begin from below, that is, from Jesus' humanity—his human words and deeds.[18] Only his authentic, historical words and actions reveal his divine personhood, that is, the truth of the Incarna-

---

[17] Within Process Christology, for example, redemption is limited to Jesus' good example which stimulates to a higher intensity the already existing redemptive process. However, under this theory, Jesus did nothing that differs in kind from what anyone else does; he just did it better. Cf. D. Griffin, *A Process Christology* (Philadelphia: Westminster, 1973), 113-48. For responses to Process Soteriology, cf. Donald Bloesch, "Process Theology in Reformed Perspective," *Listening* 14 (1979) 185-95; Weinandy, 150-52.

Francis Martin posits that a true New Testament understanding of imitating Christ involves more than human modeling but demands the work of the Spirit in a person's life. Cf. "Historical Criticism and New Testament Teaching on the Imitation of Christ," *Anthropotes* 6 (1990) 261-87.

[18] For a mature example of Christology from below, see Edward Schillebeeckx, *Jesus: An Experiment in Christology* (New York: Seabury Press, 1979).

tion. Not without significance did the centurion in Mark's Gospel proclaim Jesus to be the Son of God at the moment of his death (Mk 15:39). Here, where the humanity of Jesus was most fully evident, the divinity of Jesus was most fully revealed. The Gospel of John is clear on this point. While John's Gospel most explicitly portrays the divinity of Jesus, this revelation came exclusively through the weakness of his humanity (*sarx*): "When you have lifted up the Son of Man, then you will know that I am he" (Jn 8:28). Through Jesus' human obedience and humility, we see the glory of the only-begotten Son. As incarnate, the eternal Son never said or did anything *qua* God, but always *qua* man. To have done otherwise would have been contrary to the very truth of the Incarnation.

Even for Jesus himself, as we stated above, we can properly speak of a Christology "from below". Only within his authentic human experience (within the confines of his human "I") did he come to know the Father and the Father's will for him, and thus only within his human experience did he become conscious of and was he able to articulate his unique, divine, filial relationship. The Spirit, in and through Jesus' human prayer, study of Scripture, and obedience, brought him to conscious awareness and knowledge (within his human "I") that he was the only Son of the Father.

Here, we are able to make a distinction that is frequently overlooked in contemporary Christology. Christology "from below" always pertains to a "coming to know." It is epistemological or gnoseological in nature. That is, we come to know Jesus and what he did from below only from his human words and deeds. Jesus came to know, within the Incarnation, who he was and what he was about only through the processes of his human mind and consciousness. Thus Christology "from below" is never concerned with ontology as if Jesus *became* divine "from below," that is, that the man Jesus became more and more divine as he grew in wisdom, age, and grace.

Ontologically, the Incarnation is always "from above." The Word became flesh and not the flesh became Word (cf. Jn 1:14). The Incarnation originated in the will of the Father, the sender of the Son into the world, and was accomplished through the power of the Holy Spirit, through whom the Word took flesh in the womb of Mary (cf. Lk 1-2). Only because the Word *came to be* flesh (from above) can we come *to know* the Son of God (from below) as man. For the sake of clarity and truth, we must distinguish the gnoseological nature of Christology "from below" from the ontological nature of Christology "from above."[19]

****

We wish to show now in the remainder of this study that because the Son assumed a genuine humanity and spoke and acted in the integrity of his humanity, he transformed in kind our relationship to God and with others and, concurrently, radically transformed us.

---

[19] Hans Küng provides a clear example both of the necessity of Christology's properly beginning from below and of the confusion stemming from our coming to know Jesus from below and the "Incarnation's" being from below. See his *On Being A Christian* (Garden City, NY: Doubleday, 1796), 436-50.

E. Krasevac, O.P., is correct in saying: "If a 'Christology from below' stops, as it were, with the 'low' Christology of an early New Testament tradition (a Christology which does not fully recognize the perfect divinity of Christ), it is to be faulted for failing to carry through consistently its own method to its full historical term. The primary purpose, again, of a 'Christology from below' is to *understand* the 'high' Christology of the mature Christian confession of faith in terms of its histocial development." In his "'Christology From Above' And 'Christology From Below'", *The Thomist* 51 (1987) 299-306.

CHAPTER TWO

THE THESIS—ASSUMING OUR SINFUL FLESH

A principle forcefully echoing through all the centuries that has guided all orthodox Christology is: "What is not assumed is not saved."[1] Under this reasoning, the Church has consistently proclaimed and defended the full humanity of Christ. When the Son of God became man, he took upon himself a true material body (against the Docetists). He possessed a human soul with a human mind and will (against the Apollinarians, Monophysites, and Monothelitists).[2]

While Christian theologians have stressed that the Son of God became like us in every way, what they have almost

---

[1] While this is a common argument among the early Fathers of the Church against Docetism and Apollinarianism: Hippolytus, Tertullian, and Origen (See Aloys Grillmeier, *Christ in Christian Tradition,* Vol. 1 (Atlanta: John Knox Press, 1975), 52, 115, 148) it was Gregory of Nazianzen who gave it its classic and definitive form. "If anyone has put his trust in him (Christ) as man without a human mind, he is really bereft of mind, and quite unworthy of salvation. For that which he has not assumed, he has not healed (*to gar aproslepton, atherapeuton*); but that which is united to his Godhead is also saved. If only half Adam fell, then that which Christ assumes and saves may be half also; but if the whole of his nature fell, it must be united to the whole nature of him that was begotten, and so be saved as a whole" *Epistolae,* 101; see Or. 1.13; 30.21 (Quoted from *Christology of the Later Fathers,* ed. E. Hardy (Philadelphia: Westminster Press, 1954), 218-19.

[2] For the history of these controversies and the Church's response to them, see *ibid.* See also, J.N.D. Kelly, *Early Christian Doctrine,* (London: Adam & Charles Black, 1968); Weinandy, xix-66.

17

universally neglected and ignored, both in the present and the past, is that in the Incarnation, the Son took upon himself, not some generic humanity, but our own sinful humanity.[3] While he never sinned personally, or, as we will see, had an inner propensity to sin (concupiscence), nonetheless his humanity was of the race of Adam and he experienced, of necessity, many of the effects of sin which permeate the world and plague human beings—hunger and thirst, sickness and sorrow, temptation and harassment by Satan, being hated and despised, fear and loneliness, even death and separation from God. The eternal Son of God functioned from within the confines of a humanity altered by sin and the Fall. "He was both God and the son of Eve."[4] This then is what we mean, when throughout this study, we speak of "Jesus' sinful humanity," his "sinful flesh," or his "sinful human nature."

This perception of Jesus' human nature is absolutely essential if we are to appreciate truly the Incarnation and if we are to comprehend clearly what Jesus accomplished, in and through his humanity, on the cross, and in his resurrection. Ultimately, our salvation is unconditionally dependent upon the Son's

---

[3] Thomas V. Morris argues for a generic understanding of the humanity of Christ. He believes that such an understanding will make the humanity of Christ more compatible with his divinity. See his *The Logic of God Incarnate*. For a critique, see Thomas Weinandy's book review, *The Thomist* 51:2 (1987) 367-72.

The New Testament authors do not speak in philosophical terms, using such terms as "person" and "nature" when describing Jesus, unlike the Fathers of the Church, the early Councils, and the later Scholastics. The language and concepts of the New Testament authors were more descriptive, functional, and relational. Cf. O. Cullmann, *The Christology of the New Testament*, and R.H. Fuller, *The Foundations of New Testament Christology*, 243-59. Nonetheless, as we will see, the New Testament does attribute to Jesus all those aspects which are in accord with authentic humanness.

[4] From an ancient homily on Holy Saturday, P.G. 439.

assuming a humanity disfigured by sin and freely acting as a son of Adam.

PART TWO:

JESUS' SINFUL HUMANITY:
AN HISTORICAL OVERVIEW

A brief survey of the history of Christology, especially the patristic history and a select, few, medieval and contemporary authors, would be helpful before exploring our thesis in light of the New Testament. While an extensive study is beyond our scope here, we want to discern what evidence we may find within the history of Christology and soteriology which would found, advance, and confirm our proposition that Jesus was born of the fallen race of Adam and that such a condition was absolutely indispensable for our salvation.

We espouse as our own one of the criteria John Henry Cardinal Newman set forth for judging genuine development, that of "Anticipation of Its Future:"

> The fact, then, of such early or recurring intimations or tendencies which afterwards are fully realized is a sort of evidence that those later and more systematic fulfillments are only in accordance with the original idea.[1]

Are there any intimations within the history of Christology which would lend themselves to a development within the Church's tradition concerning Jesus' sinful humanity?

---

[1] *An Essay on the Development of Christian Doctrine* (Garden City, NY: Image Books, 1960), 198.

CHAPTER THREE

JESUS' HUMANITY:
PATRISTIC CHRISTOLOGY

This chapter addresses the issue of how patristic Christology understood the humanity of Jesus, specifically, whether the Fathers of the Church anticipated our thesis, thus providing support for it. This examination will not be exhaustive by any means, but rather quite selective. Nonetheless, we hope, within this brief chapter, to detect the various currents which bear upon our inquiry.

Since no patristic treatises specifically address the question of whether or not Jesus possessed a humanity tainted by the sin of Adam, we cannot obtain an exact picture of what the various Fathers believed about this, if they indeed had an opinion. The evidence concerning the precise nature of Jesus' humanity forms part of the broader christological issues of their day—the relationship between person(s) and natures—and is intertwined with the challenges they encountered—Docetism, Apollinarianism, Nestorianism, and Monophysitism. Nonetheless, relevant testimony is available which allows us to determine, if not always precisely, the Fathers' fundamental posture and the direction in which their christological thought was advancing.

Two Who Say No

Clement of Alexandria (150-215) took a view of Jesus' humanity that would definitely place him in opposition to the present thesis. Heavily influenced by Stoic philosophy, Clement did not allow even the most ordinary of human tribulations and appetites to touch Jesus:

> For he ate, not because of bodily needs, since his body was supported by holy power, but so that his companions might not entertain a false notion about him, as in fact certain men did later, namely that he had been manifested only in appearance. He himself was, and remained, "untroubled by passion"; no movement of the passions, either pleasure or pain, found its way into him.[2]

While Clement wished to uphold the true humanity of Jesus, his argument throws his defense into question. How could Jesus' humanity be more than mere pretense if he only appeared to be eating, suffering, etc.?

Hilary of Poitiers (315-367), while not as extreme as Clement, held similar reservations about attributing to Jesus the full weight of human weakness. His humanity, though real, was heavenly in origin. Hilary thus conceded that Jesus truly wept, thirsted, and hungered in the flesh, but Hilary would not allow actual suffering:[3]

> The ordinary behavior of the body was accepted to show the reality of his body. . . . When he took drink and food, he did not submit himself to bodily necessity, but to customary bodily behavior. He had a body, but one appropriate to its origin; not owing its being to the faults of human conception, but existing in the form of our body by his divine

---

[2] *Stromateis,* 6.9 (71). All translations from the Fathers are taken from either of Henry Bettenson's editions: *The Early Christian Fathers* (Oxford: University Press, 1956); *The Later Christian Fathers* (Oxford: University Press, 1970), unless otherwise stated.

[3] Cf. *De Trinitate,* 10.23.

power. He bore the form of a servant, but he was free from the sins and weaknesses of a human body.[4]

The Reality of Jesus' Humanity

Clement's and Hilary's views were in the minority. Faced with the challenge of Docetism (which accorded to Jesus only the appearance and not the reality of humanness), and later with Apollinarianism (which denied that Jesus possessed a human soul), the Fathers did not hesitate to assert the true and full humanity of Jesus. As early as Ignatius of Antioch (d.107), we find a rousing defense of Jesus' humanity: "Turn a deaf ear to any speaker who avoids mention of Jesus Christ who was of David's line, born of Mary, who was truly born, ate and drank; was truly persecuted under Pontius Pilate, truly crucified and died."[5]

Ignatius was confronting Docetism and not addressing the question of whether Jesus possessed a humanity scarred by sin. Nonetheless, already here, we perceive two foundational arguments for such a development—Jesus' sin-marred lineage (David's line) and the reality of his suffering and death.

In the fourth century, Cyril of Jerusalem (315-386) emphasized the reality of Jesus' humanity:

Believe also that he, the only begotten Son of God, for our sins came down to earth from heaven, assuming a manhood subject to the same feelings as ours, and being born of a holy virgin and the Holy Spirit: and this not in appearance or in imagination, but in reality. He did not pass through the Virgin as through a channel, but truly took flesh and was truly fed with milk from her. He truly ate as we eat, and

---

[4] *Ibid.*, 10.24,25.
[5] *Letter to the Trallians*, 9. See also, *The Letter to the Smyrnaeans*, 1-4.

drank as we drink. For if the incarnation was a figment then our salvation was a figment.[6]

Here, we again see the genesis of an important line of argument which would expand and deepen throughout the patristic era. The reality of our salvation is predicated upon the reality of the Incarnation. The Son of God truly had to become as we are, and, as man, die for us, so as to obtain for us genuine salvation.

Jesus' Human Weakness

The orthodox response to the challenge of Docetism and Apollinarianism also necessitated a focusing on Jesus' human weaknesses. Irenaeus (130-200) and Origen (185-254) acknowledged that he was truly tempted. Irenaeus wrote: "As he was man that he might be tempted, so he was the Word that he might be glorified." While Irenaeus attributed this weakness not only to his humanity, but also to the "quietness" of being the Word, nonetheless, Jesus was capable of temptation, dishonor, crucifixion, and death.[7] Origen recorded that Jesus took our flesh and so was tempted in every way as we so that he might obtain victory for us.[8]

Moreover, Origen and Athanasius (296-373) recognized Jesus' limited human knowledge. Athanasius argued: "The all holy Word of God bore our ignorance so that he might bestow on us the knowledge of God." Or again, "Since he was made man he is not ashamed to profess ignorance because of the

---

[6] *Catecheses*, 4.9. Origen also stressed the reality of Jesus' human nature: "When he took upon him the nature of human flesh, he fully accepted all the characteristic properties of humanity, so that it be realized that he had a body of flesh in reality and not in mere appearance." *In Matthaeum Commentariorum Series*, 92.

[7] *Adversus Haereses*, III,19,3.

[8] See *Homiliae: In Lucam*, 29.

ignorance of flesh; to show that though knowing as God he is ignorant according to the flesh."[9]

What Is Not Assumed Is Not Healed

However, did the Fathers believe, or at least suggest, that the weaknesses of Jesus' flesh were evidence for his possessing not merely a generic humanity of the same species as ours, but a humanity inherited from and tarnished by sinful Adam?

Irenaeus stated that we could become adopted sons of God only if;

> the Word of God made flesh had entered into communion with us. . . . For he who was to destroy sin and redeem man from guilt had to enter into the very condition of man, who had been dragged into slavery and was held by death, in order that death might be slain by man, and man should go forth from the bondage of death.[10]

Cyril of Jerusalem believed that Jesus "took on our likeness" so that our "sinful human nature might become partaker of God."[11]

Irenaeus also argued that Jesus in his humanity "summed up" and embodied all the sinful generations since Adam so that he might redeem every generation.[12] Gregory of Nazianzus (329-389) similarly affirmed, maintaining the principle that what is not assumed is not saved: "If it was half of Adam that

---

[9] Athanasius, *Contra Arianos,* 3.38,43. See also, Origen, *In Matthaeum Commentariorum Series,* 55. The majority of the Fathers admitted that, *as man,* Jesus did not know the last day. Augustine spoke of Jesus also experiencing weariness. See *Homiliae in Joannis Evangelium,* 15.6.

[10] *Adversus Haereses,* III,18,7. See II,12,4; III,18,1.

[11] *Catecheses,* 12.15.

[12] See *Adversus Haereses,* III,21,10; III,12,3.

fell, then half might be assumed and saved. But if it was the whole of Adam that fell, it is united to the whole of him who was begotten, and gains complete salvation."[13]

What we see emerging here is the principal soteriological argument that this study embraces and employs. Only if Jesus assumed a humanity at one with the fallen race of Adam could his death and resurrection heal and save that humanity. While the Fathers, as we will see shortly, protected Jesus from personal sin and from the morally debilitating consequences of Adam's sin, they nonetheless were adamant that his nature derived from Adam's sin-gnarled family tree.

Irenaeus proclaimed a truth that would reverberate ever more loudly throughout patristic Christology: "Our Lord Jesus Christ, the word of God, of his boundless love, became what we are that he might make us what he himself is."[14] Tertullian (160-220) wrote: "God lived with men as man that man might be taught to live the divine life: God lived on man's level, that man might be able to live on God's level: God was found weak, that man might become most great."[15] He also argued that Jesus did not despise humiliation, birth, suffering, death, but rather out of love, he sanctified the whole of human life for if he did not do so, then man is not redeemed.[16] Athanasius professed: "We should not have been freed from sin and the curse, had not the flesh which the Word assumed been by nature human."[17] Again, "The Word was made man in order that we might be made divine."[18] Gregory of Nazianzus

---

[13] *Epistolae,* 101.7.

[14] *Adversus Haereses,* V. preaf.

[15] *Adversus Marcionem,* 2.27.

[16] See *De Carne Christi,* 4-6. See also Athanasius, *Contra Arianos,* 3.33,57.

[17] *Contra Arianos,* 2.70.

[18] *De Incarnatione,* 54.

stated: "He shares in my flesh in order that he may rescue the image and confer immortality on the flesh. . . . He imparted an honor; now he shares a humiliation."[19] Augustine (354-430) too argued: "For assuredly God could have taken upon himself to be man. . .from some other source, and not from the race of Adam who bound the human race by his sin. . . . But God judged it better both to take upon him man through whom to conquer the enemy of the human race, from the race itself that had been conquered; and yet to do this of a virgin, whose conception, not flesh but spirit, not lust but faith, preceded."[20] Again, "Never would you have been freed from sinful flesh, had he not taken on himself the likeness of sinful flesh."[21] Or, "The Son of God assumed human nature, and in it he endured all that belongs to the human condition. This is a remedy for mankind of a power beyond our imagining."[22] Or, "He therefore [was made] sin, as we [were made] justice; not our justice, but that of God; not in ourselves, but in him; just as he [was made] sin, not his own sin, but our sin."[23]

These passages reveal that only by the eternal Son's assumption of our humanity, a humanity that sin defiled and infected, is our humanity healed, renewed, and given immortality. Even if some passages do not absolutely affirm this, they firmly assert a principle that forcefully advances that conclusion: "What is not assumed is not saved."

For example, Ambrosiaster argued very strongly on behalf of Jesus' "sinful flesh:"

---

[19] *Orationes,* 38.13.
[20] *De Trinitate,* 13.18. Translation from *Nicene and Post-Nicene Fathers,* Vol. III, ed. Philip Schaff (Grand Rapids: Eerdmans, 1978 repr.).
[21] *Sermo,* 185.
[22] *De Agone Christiano,* 12.
[23] *Enchiridion,* 41. Translated from *Enchiridion Patristicum,* 1916.

"Him who did not know sin, he made sin on our behalf." It says that God the Father made his Son, Christ, sin; because having been made flesh he was not altered but became incarnate and so was made sin. . . . On account of this his entire flesh is under sin, therefore since it has been made flesh, it has also been made sin. And since he has been offered for sin, not undeservedly is he said to have been made sin; since also a victim which was offered for sins under the law was named sin.[24]

What is of special interest here is that Ambrosiaster clearly affirmed that the Son took on our sin within the Incarnation itself, in the assuming of our flesh, and thus that his flesh, too, "is under sin." The cross then, the offering of the victim, is a consequence of the Incarnation itself.[25]

Yet Without Sin

The above passages, while they encourage the thesis that Jesus partook of Adam's fallen nature, represent only half of the argument. The corollary is that only because Jesus never personally sinned within the confines of our sinful condition did he bring us salvation.

---

[24] *In ad Corinthios Secunda,* 5,21. Translated from the *Enchiridion Patristicum,* 1342.

[25] T.F. Torrance in his excellent book, *The Trinitarian Faith* (Edinburgh: T. & T. Clark, 1988), also finds support among many of the Fathers for holding that Jesus assumed a humanity from the sinful race of Adam. He writes, for example, of Athanasius: "Thus Athanasius could say that 'the whole Christ became a curse for us', for in taking upon himself the form of a servant, the Lord transferred to himself fallen Adamic humanity which he took from the Virgin Mary, that is, our perverted, corrupt, degenerate, diseased human nature enslaved to sin and subject to death under the condemnation of God" (p. 161). See Athanasius *Contra Arianos,* 1.43,51,60; 2.14,47,55,66,69; 3.31. For further quotations from the Fathers and commentary see Torrance, pp. 161-68.

Tertullian stated the whole argument concisely:

> Our contention, however, is not that the flesh of sin, but that the sin of the flesh, was brought to nought in Christ, not the material but its quality, not the substance but its guilt, according to the apostle's authority when he says, "He brought to nought sin in the flesh." For in another place also he says that Christ was in the likeness of the flesh of sin: not that he took upon him the likeness of flesh, as it were a phantasm of a body and not its reality: but the apostle will have us understand by "the likeness of sinful flesh" that the flesh of Christ, itself not sinful, was the like of that to which sin did belong, and is to be equated with Adam in species but not in defect. From this text we also prove that in Christ there was that flesh whose nature is in man sinful, and it is by virtue of this that sin has been brought to naught, while in Christ that same flesh exists without sin which in man did not exist without sin. Moreover it would not suit Christ's purpose, when bringing to nought the sin of the flesh, not to bring it to nought in that flesh in which was the nature of sin: neither would it be to his glory. For what would it amount to if it was in a better kind of flesh, of a different (that is, a non-sinful) nature, that he destroyed the birthmark of sin? "In that case," you will reply, "if it was our flesh Christ clothed himself with, Christ's flesh was sinful." Forebear to tie up tight a conception which admits of unravelling. By clothing himself with our flesh he made it his own, and by making it his own he made it non-sinful.[26]

Tertullian asserted three truths here. Firstly, Jesus possessed a real and not a phantasmal humanity. Secondly, he did not

---

[26] *De Carne Christi,* 16,10-25. Translation from Ernest Evans, Tertullian's *Treatise on the Incarnation* (London: SPCK, 1956), 57.

assume a "better kind" of flesh, but one like our own that bore the "birthmark of sin". Only by taking such a humanity did he suit his purposes of healing and salvation. Thirdly, while he thus was in the likeness of sinful flesh bearing our guilt and shame, sin did not interiorly touch (in "substance") him and he did not sin personally. Only as we hold these truths in communion is salvation guaranteed.

In a similar manner, Basil the Great (330-379) stressed that Jesus suffered the weakness of the flesh, but did not experience that which "arises from wickedness." He assumed the likeness of sinful flesh "with its natural experiences, but 'he did not sin'. Just as the death which is in the flesh has been transmitted to us through Adam, and was swallowed up by the godhead, so the sinfulness was annulled by the righteousness which is in Christ Jesus."[27] Ambrose (339-397) declared: "He took flesh like ours, of the same substance as our flesh. He was indeed a perfect man, but without any stain of sin."[28]

Augustine also is very clear on this two-fold truth. While Jesus was born of Adam, he was not born with concupiscence.[29] Augustine would even go so far as to say, seemingly in contradiction to what we previously quoted, that Jesus "is not a branch derived from Adam: flesh only did he derive from Adam, Adam's sin he did not assume. He who took not upon him sin from our lump, he it is who taketh away sin."[30] However, what Augustine wished to preserve was Jesus' separation from us as to sin, not separation from us as to the flesh.

---

[27] *Epistolae*, 261.3.

[28] *De Incarnationis Dominicae Sacramento*, 76. See also *Expositio In Psalmum*, 118.6,22.

[29] See *Homiliae In Joannis Evangelium*, 3.12.

[30] *Ibid.*, 4.10. See also ibid., 41.5; 43.9. Translations for Augustine's *Commentary on the Gospel of John* are from *Nicene and Post-Nicene Fathers of the Christian Church*, Vol. VII, ed. Philip Schaff (Grand Rapids: Eerdmans, 1978).

All of humanity is one with Adam, but "in Christ he is being renewed: because an Adam is come without sin, to destroy the sin of Adam in his own flesh and that Adam might renew to himself the image of God. Of Adam then is Christ's flesh: of Adam the temple which the Jews destroyed, and the Lord raised up in three days."[31] Thus for Augustine, Christ came in the "likeness" of sinful flesh, but not in sinful flesh, "because he had not sin at all; and therefore became a true sacrifice for sin, because he himself had no sin."[32]

Not surprisingly, what could and could not be predicated of Jesus reached a new and heightened intensity in the context of the Nestorian controversy. The question of whether or not Mary could be called *Theotokos* had obvious and significant repercussions about what could or could not be predicated about her son. All combatants—Nestorius (d.451) and the Antiochenes, Theodore of Mopsuestia (350-428) and Theodoret of Cyrus (393-458), as well as Cyril of Alexandria (d.444)—professed the reality of Jesus' humanity with all its weaknesses.[33] For Nestorius, this was precisely the problem. If Jesus' humanity was subject to change, weakness, temptation, suffering, and death, then such attributes could not be predicated of the Son for as God he was unchangeable, holy, and perfect. However, what for Nestorius was an unthinkable, intolerable scandal was, for Cyril of Alexandria, the Incarnation's glory.

Echoing the tradition, Cyril repeatedly stressed with majesty and boldness: "If the Word had not been begotten,

---

[31] *Ibid.*, 10.11.

[32] *Ibid.*, 41,5. See also John Chrysostom, *Homiliae In Epistulam Secundam Ad Corinthios*, XI,5,21.

[33] See Theodore of Mopsuestia, *Homiliae Catecheticae*, 5.9-11; 8.1. See also Nestorius, *Liber Heracleidis*, trs. R.C. Driver and L. Hodgson (Oxford: Clarendon Press, 1925), 8-9; Theodoret of Cyrus, *Reprehensio XII Capitum seu Anathematismorum Cyrilli*, 3.

according to the flesh, in the same way as we are, if he had not shared in our condition in this way, he would not have freed human nature from the guilt we inherit from Adam, nor have driven away the corruption from our bodies."[34] Commenting on Heb 2:14 and Rom 8:3, Cyril acknowledged that it is "obvious" that the eternal Son became "identical with us, in respect of the conditions of life."[35] He could take upon himself our curse only if he was born in our condition, "numbered among transgressors."[36] The Word took on the reality of our humanity blemished by sin that "he might annihilate sin, and put an end to Satan's accusations: for in the person of Christ himself he paid the penalty of the sins of which we stood accused."[37] Cyril was also very much aware that, though the Word had become like us, yet as man, he did not personally know transgression.[38]

Cyril's statements bore the acerbity of his passionate personality as well as the intensity of conflict, but this fervor heightened the soteriological nature of his arguments. Cyril was convinced that the eternal Word of God actually came to exist as man and as man he truly endured the weaknesses, tribulations, and sufferings that are endemic in man because of sin, so that as man he could freely and righteously vanquish them, thus winning our salvation.

The Council of Chalcedon (451) did not specifically address the question of whether or not Jesus possessed a human-

---

[34] *Adversus Nestorii Blasphemias,* 1.1. See also, *ibid.,* 3.2; *Epistolae Ad Nestorius,* 2.

[35] *Scholia de Incarnatione Unigeniti,* 2. See also *Quod Unus Sit Christus,* tr., *St. Cyril of Alexandria: On the Incarnation Against Nestorius,* Library of the Fathers (Oxford: James Parker, 1881), 293, 300-301.

[36] *Quod Unus Sit Christus,* tr., 243-44. See also *Scholia de Incarnatione Unigeniti,* 12.

[37] *De Adoratione in Spiritu et Veritate,* 3.

[38] See *Quod Unus Sit Christus,* tr., 276.

ity of Adam's sinful lineage. However, contrary to Eutyches' Monophysitism, which would have strongly endorsed an uncontaminated humanity because Jesus' divinity sanitized it, the Fathers of Chalcedon professed that the person of the one, eternal Son was not only *homoousios* with the Father, but also *homoousios* with us in his humanity, "like us in every way except sin."[39] This *homoousios* doctrine propels Christology in the direction of our thesis, for to be *homoousios* with us demands more than a generic, ahistorical sameness of species, but a communion with us as we are in reality—brothers and sisters defiled by the sin of Adam.

Pope Leo the Great (d.461) in his Tome to Flavian, which the Council of Chalcedon confirmed, contains the principal points of our study thus far. Leo contended that the Word did not withdraw from his divinity or "desert the nature of our kind:"

> For we could not overcome the author of sin and death, unless he [Jesus] had taken our nature, and made it his own, whom sin could not defile nor death retain. . . . Thus the properties of each nature and substance were preserved entire, and came together to form one person. Humility was

[39] Denzinger-Schonmetzer, 301, 302.
Bishop Julian of Halicarnassus in the sixth century held what Leontius of Byzantium believed was Monophysitism *par excellence,* that is, in all its logical consequences. Julian asserted that Jesus' humanity, so purified of sin and shielded from its effects, was incorruptible, impassible, and immortal from birth (*Aphthartodocetae*). Even the more moderate Monophysites, such as Severus of Antioch, argued against him. See Leontius of Byzantium, *Contra Nestorianos et Eutychianos,* II; John Meyendorff, *Christ in Eastern Christian Thought* (New York: St. Vladimir's Press, 1975), 88-89; John Meyendorff, *Byzantine Theology* (New York: Fordham University Press, 1979), 157-58;. R.V. Sellers, *The Council of Chalcedon* (London: SPCK, 1961), 309-10 fn. 6.

assumed by majesty, weakness by strength, mortality by eternity; and to pay the debt that we had incurred, an inviolable nature was united to a nature that can suffer. . . . Thus there was born true God in the entire and perfect nature of true man, complete in his own properties, complete in ours. By "ours" I mean those which the Creator formed in us at the beginning, which he assumed in order to restore; for in the Savior there was no trace of the properties which the deceiver brought in, and which man, being deceived, allowed to enter. He did not become partaker of our sins because he entered into fellowship with human infirmities. He assumed the form of a servant without the stain of sin.[40]

In order to protect the reality and concepts of Jesus' holiness and our salvation, Leo placed greater emphasis on Jesus' dissimilarity with our nature, but without denying the essential similarity. Leo did not hesitate to declare that when the Son "lowered himself to our condition, he not only assumed our substance (nature), but also the condition of our sinfulness."[41]

---

[40] *Epistola Dogmatica Ad Flavianum,* 2-4.

[41] Translated from St. Leo the Great, *Sermo* 7:2.

In the midst of the Monothelite controversy (634), Pope Honorius I declared: "Therefore we also confess one will of our Lord Jesus Christ, because indeed our nature was assumed by divinity but not our fault. Indeed that nature was assumed which was created before sin, and not that which was defiled after the prevarication [*illa profecto, quae ante peccatum creata est, non quae post praevaricationem vitiata*]. For Christ was conceived by the Holy Spirit without sin, and also was born separated from sin of the holy and immaculate Virgin Mother of God. For another law is in our members; however the Savior did not have a contrary or diverse will, because he was born above the law of the human condition" (Denzinger-Schonmetzer, 487).

In this historically controversial statement, Honorius is obviously stating that the human and divine wills of Christ are always in mutual

A Two-fold Conclusion

In concluding, we want to re-emphasize the soteriological nature of the Fathers' arguments. Within the Incarnation, the Son of God must have been a man like us, since he was to heal and save our fallen nature, and yet, as one of us, he must not have experienced the moral corruption of sin either within his nature or in his personal choices: he did not sin. The Fathers, depending upon which aspect of this two-fold soteriological truth they wished to uphold, stressed either one or the other. Firstly, when arguing that it was only through Jesus' holy and innocent life—his obedience and the free offering of himself to the Father on the cross—that we are saved, they emphasized his dissimilarity to us as man. He knew no corruption of sin. Secondly and conversely, as they professed that Jesus redeemed and saved our fallen nature, they accentuated the likeness of Jesus' humanity to our own—a son of Adam as to his flesh. This two-fold soteriological thrust brought both ambiguity and tension within patristic Christology. Yet the Fathers recognized, consciously and sometimes not, that both must be maintained.

The inherited patristic tradition, even to our own day, has more firmly and consistently espoused and developed the first

---

agreement and thus they form one common will or accord. The whole point of making Jesus' humanity pre-lapsarian was to assure that there would be nothing sinful within his humanity that would foster friction and induce conflict between the human and the divine wills.

However, does this authoritative statement then condemn the position we advance here—that Jesus possessed a post-lapsarian nature? Since it was Honorius' primary intention to uphold the harmony of wills within Christ and not to make a definitive statement on the nature of Jesus' humanity, it would seem not. The unanimity of Jesus' divine and human wills is not absolutely dependent upon his having possessed a pre-lapsarian humanity. We argue to the contrary that only if Jesus possessed a humanity tainted by sin would his human will have had any real and efficacious salvific value.

principle, at times, to the detriment of the second. This study, without denying the absolute necessity of Jesus' sinlessness, wishes to demonstrate that his assuming a humanity that bore the birthmark of sin is of equal importance. Actually, only as the Son inherited an enfeebled humanity does his sinless life possess any soteriological value.

CHAPTER FOUR

JESUS' HUMANITY:
MEDIEVAL CHRISTOLOGY

St. Anselm

St. Anselm (1033-1109) may well be the first theologian who addressed directly the question our study treats. His concern about the nature of Jesus' humanity formed an integral part of his soteriology. He first discussed the topic of Jesus' "sinful" humanity in his *Cur Deus Homo* and later and more specifically in light of his previous teaching in *De Conceptu Virginali et de Originali Peccato*.

In *Cur Deus Homo*, Anselm argued, contrary to the accusations of unbelievers and pagans, that God's becoming man was not unfitting. For him, the unbelievable happened—the omnipotent God assumed "the littleness and weakness of human nature for the sake of its renewal."[1] Anselm neither denied nor shunned the truth that God "descended into the womb of a virgin...that he grew on the nourishment of milk and the food of men; and passing over many other things which seem incompatible with Deity, that he endured fatigue, hunger, thirst, stripes and crucifixion among thieves."[2] Anselm founded his entire soteriology upon the premise that not only

---

[1] *Cur Deus Homo*, I,2. Translation from *St. Anselm: Basic Writings*, S.N. Deane (La Salle: Open Court Press, 1968).
[2] *Ibid.*, I,3.

did the Incarnation not dishonor God, but also it was absolutely indispensable for our salvation.[3]

One of Adam's Sinful Race

Without addressing the debatable details and merits of Anselm's
soteriology, we can see that the basic premises are relevant to
our study. For Anselm, once man had sinned, he was unable
to restore himself to a condition in which he could properly
give God the honor and the love he deserved. Nevertheless,
since it was man who sinned, the obligation for restoring God's
honor fell directly upon man's shoulders. But man in his sinful
state could not fulfill that obligation. Man's sin so violated the
honor of God that only God himself could restore and make
satisfaction for the loss. Anselm believed that sin had created
a situation in which "None but God can make satisfaction. .
.but none but a man ought to do this."[4]

Only a person who was both God and man could overcome
this dilemma. As Anselm stated: "If it is necessary, therefore,
as it appears, that the heavenly kingdom be made up of men,
and this cannot be effected unless the aforesaid satisfaction be
made, which none but God can make and none but man ought
to make, it is necessary for the God-man to make it."[5] How-

---

[3] J. Hopkins is correct: "In a sense, the entire *Cur Deus Homo* is directed
towards proving this thesis [that the Son had to become man for our
salvation]. Anselm thinks that if he can show the impossibility of human
redemption's occurring other than through the agency of a God-man, he
will have removed the stigma which seems to accompany the notion of
incarnation." *A Companion to the Study of St. Anselm* (Minneapolis:
University of Minnesota Press, 1972), 187. See also, J. McIntyre, *St.
Anselm and His Critics* (London, 1954), 127.

[4] *Cur Deus Homo*, II,6. See also, ibid. I,11; I,23.

[5] *Ibid.;* also II,15. Anselm's soteriology demands a Chalcedonian
understanding of the Incarnation. See I,8; II,7; II,9. See also Weinandy,
67-71.

ever, what type of man must the Son of God have to become if he were to render satisfaction on our behalf?

Since Adam was and his children are responsible for dishonoring God and so are accountable for making satisfaction, Anselm found it imperative that the Son become as we are. Jesus had to possess a humanity sprung from the sinful root of Adam:

> For he [the Son] will either take it [human nature] from Adam, or else he will make a new man, as he made Adam originally. But, if he makes a new man, not of Adam's race, then this man will not belong to the human family, which descended from Adam, and therefore ought not to make atonement for it, because he never belonged to it. For, as it is right for man to make atonement for the sin of man, it is also necessary that he who makes the atonement should be the very being who has sinned, or else one of the same race. Otherwise, neither Adam nor his race would make satisfaction for themselves. Therefore, as through Adam and Eve sin was propagated among all men, so none but themselves, or one born of them, ought to make atonement for the sin of men. And, since they cannot, one born of them must fulfill this work. . . . Wherefore, if the race of Adam be reinstated by any being not of the same race, it will not be restored to that dignity which it would have had, had not Adam sinned, and so will not be completely restored; and, besides God will seem to have failed of his purpose, both of which suppositions are incongruous. It is, therefore, necessary that the man by whom Adam's race shall be restored be taken from Adam.[6]

---

[6] *Ibid.*, II,8.

No argument to date has so clearly and forcefully affirmed that the Son of God must have assumed a humanity of Adam's sinful lineage for to have done otherwise would have been inefficacious.

Though Sinless

However, Anselm is equally clear that Jesus must have been sinless for only in the offering of his holy and innocent life was full and true satisfaction made to the Father.[7] Jesus was free of original sin and its subsequent concupiscence.[8] Anselm advanced his argument even further, stating that since Jesus was sinless, there was no inherent necessity that he die, for mortality is due to sin.[9]   Rather, Jesus offered his life on the cross, not because of the compulsion of debt (he was not a debtor as we are), but freely and voluntarily:

> Now, nothing can be more severe or difficult for man to do for God's honor, than to suffer death voluntarily when not bound by obligation; and man cannot give himself to God in any way more truly than by surrendering himself to death for God's honor.[10]

Anselm attempted to preserve and enhance the significance of Jesus' sacrifice, but in so doing, did he undermine the very premise upon which his soteriology was based—the requirement that Jesus be of our sinful stock? Can Jesus be truly like us in any genuine sense if his suffering and death were not inherent within the humanity he assumed? Granted Jesus was

[7] See *ibid.*, I,9; II,11; II,20.

[8] See *ibid.*, II,16.

[9] *Ibid.*, II,11. Anselm also professed that Jesus was devoid of ignorance since he possessed all good. See ibid., II,13.

[10] *Ibid.*

not a debtor in the sense that sin morally deformed him or that he sinned personally. But was he not a debtor in that by freely and truly becoming one of us through the Incarnation, he assumed our indebtedness with its congenital suffering and death? From within our indebtedness, he then freely offered his sinless life to the Father on our behalf.

At this crucial juncture, Anselm knew that his soteriology had an inherent tension. At one and the same time, Jesus must be "taken without sin and yet of a sinful substance."[11] Thus, he asked: "How does God, from a sinful substance, that is, of human species, which was wholly tainted by sin, take a man without sin, as an unleavened lump from that which is leavened?"[12] In *Cur Deus Homo*, Anselm appealed more to faith—it happened therefore God could do it—than to theological explanation. Nonetheless, he thought that Mary's sinlessness and the conception of Jesus by the power of the Holy Spirit were the keys to a complete understanding.[13]

While continuing to adhere, at least in theory, to the absolute requisite that Jesus be the offspring of Adam, Anselm nonetheless felt obliged in *De Conceptu Virginali et de Originali Peccato* to defend vigorously the sinlessness of Jesus. In so doing, he jeopardized, in fact, Jesus' "sinful" humanity and thus the very foundation of his soteriology. Advancing and developing the arguments already set forth in *Cur Deus Homo*, Anselm so intensely and thoroughly shielded Jesus from sin and its effects that his likeness to our sinful flesh, while logically and theoretically preserved as a foundational premise to his soteriology, bore little resemblance to man in reality. Anselm

---

[11] *Ibid.*, II,16; II,18a.

[12] *Ibid.*

[13] See *ibid.*, II,16 and 18a. Anselm was aware that he did not fully treat the question at hand and thus promised to take up the topic at another time, which he did in *De Conceptu Virginali et de Originali Peccato*.

asserted that while Jesus came from the sinful mass of humanity since he was born of Mary, he did not inherit original sin with its debilitating effects. The three-fold reason that he was born in holiness possessing original justice was: (1) it was the all-holy Son of God who became man; (2) he was born of a pure and sinless virgin; and (3) he was conceived by the power of the Holy Spirit:[14]

> So we can now freely conclude that there is no reason, no truth, or no understanding which allows us to assert that anything pertaining to the sin of the sinful mass could or should have affected that man who was conceived from the Virgin alone. And this conclusion is true, even though he was assumed from that sinful mass; and it would still be true even if he were not God.[15]

Anselm, as in *Cur Deus Homo*, concluded again that Jesus being righteous and holy did not have to die: "It was only because of his holy will (and not because of any necessity) that our Lord and Redeemer took upon himself all the things which he suffered."[16]

An Unresolved Tension

In the final analysis, has Anselm truly upheld that Jesus assumed a humanity from a sinful breed? He truly perceived

---

[14] Cf. *De Conceptu Virginali et de Originali Peccato*, Prologue; 1; 7-8; 11-14.

[15] *Ibid.*, 15. Translation from *Anselm of Canterbury: Trinity, Incarnation, and Redemption*, eds. and trs. Jasper Hopkins and Herbert Richardson (New York: Harper Torch books, 1970). See also page 23. Anselm is here following St. Augustine. Jesus was born free of original sin because he was not conceived through sexual communion, but through communion with the Holy Spirit. Cf. *Enchiridion*, 41.13. See also Hopkins, 202-12.

[16] *Ibid.*, 19.

that Jesus must be of the race of Adam and strongly argued his position—the responsibility for making reparation to God rightly fell to sinful humanity. He likewise understood that Jesus must have been holy and sinless. However, in attempting to ensure that Jesus was without sin and thus holy enough to be an effective sacrifice, he subverted the very heart of his argument. If Jesus possessed original justice to such a degree that he was entirely immune to the effects of Adam's sin, if the absence of original sin so transformed his humanity that his trials, sufferings, and death were not inherent within his assumed humanity but only a consequence of his voluntary choice later (post-incarnationally), then it is difficult to see how Jesus was truly of our stock. His identity with us becomes little more than a legal fiction.

Anselm perceived rightly that Jesus freely and willingly offered his holy and sinless life to the Father. However, the merit in his sacrifice is not that he died when he was not required to do so but that, from within a humanity marred by sin and subjected to temptation and death (as is all of Adam's race), he persistently and resolutely obeyed God. As this "sinful" man, who assumed our debt when he assumed our nature, he freely offered his life to the Father. Here we want to be more Anselmian than Anselm. Truly, Jesus was free of all moral corruption in order for his sacrifice to have been efficacious, but equally he was a man who truly bore the brandmark of sin since he died for us sinful men.

Anselm did not adhere totally to his soteriological insight because his theological parameters limited him. Wanting to use reason alone in order to accommodate the unbeliever, Anselm narrowly confined his soteriological defense of the Incarnation to that of making reparation to the Father. Jesus' affinity to us became merely the logical and legal prerequisite for offering the more important and necessary reparational sacrifice. While this reasoned response was biblically inspired,

Anselm nonetheless lost the broader biblical outlook. As we will see in our study of St. Paul, Jesus needed to assume our "sinful" humanity not only to reconcile us to the Father, but also to put our sinful flesh to death. We needed to be re-created—to die and rise. This fuller scriptural perspective preserves, deepens, and enhances Anselm's legitimate, soteriological concept.[17]

[17] Before we proceed to St. Thomas Aquinas, we pause at St. Bernard of Clairvaux. Bernard possessed a deep devotion to the humanity of Jesus and the salvation Jesus won for us through his humanity. Moreover for Bernard, the humanity of Jesus is the present foundation for our ascent to God. No matter what spiritual heights we may achieve, we never leave behind this sacred humanity (cf. *On the Song of Songs,* Sermons 15, 20, 43, 61, 70). While Bernard never systematically addressed the question concerning Jesus' sin-scarred humanity, nonetheless we can find references.

For example, in his *On the Song of Songs,* commenting on the passage "I am black but beautiful" (1:4), Bernard not only perceived this as a reference to the sin and suffering of Jesus' now-righteous bride the Church, but also as an allusion to Jesus himself. Like his beloved bride, he too as the groom experienced the effects of sin and shame. For Bernard, the suffering servant songs of Deutero-Isaiah tell of Jesus' "blackness:"

> Obviously black, since he had neither beauty nor majesty; black because he was "a worm and no man, scorned by men and despised by the people." If he even made himself into sin, shall I shrink saying he was black? Look steadily at him in his filth-covered cloak, livid from blows, smeared with spittle, pale as death: surely then you must pronounce him black. . . . Beautiful in his own right, his blackness is because of you. Even clad in my form, how beautiful you are, Lord Jesus! (*Sermon,* 25:8-9).

The beauty of Jesus becomes transparent for Bernard within the blackness of our human sinful form.

Again, Bernard declared:

> It is better that one be blackened for the sake of all "in the likeness of sinful flesh," than for the whole of mankind to be lost by the blackness of sin; that the splendor and image of the substance of God should be shrouded in the form of a slave, in order that a slave might live; that the

St. Thomas Aquinas

St. Thomas Aquinas (1225-1274) also addressed directly the concerns of our study, affirming the true and full reality of Jesus' humanity.[18] Unexpectedly, at least to those who remember him primarily for professing Christ's earthly beatific vision and infused knowledge, he consistently confirmed that the Son of God assumed a humanity of the stock of sinful Adam, and thus that his humanity bore the likeness of sinful flesh.

Assuming Sinful Flesh But Not Sin

Aquinas gave three reasons for the Son's assumption of the humanity of Adam's sinful race:

> brightness of eternal light should become dimmed in the flesh for the purging of the flesh; that he who surpasses all mankind in beauty should be eclipsed by the darkness of the Passion for the enlightening of mankind; that he himself should suffer the ignominy of the cross, grow pale in death, be totally deprived of beauty and comeliness that he might gain the church as a beautiful and comely bride, without stain.

Because Jesus was like us in every way yet without personal sin, Bernard said: "I recognize here the image of our sin-darkened nature; I recognize the garments of skins that clothed our sinning first parents. He even brought his blackness on himself by assuming the condition of slave, and under the kid-skin, a symbol of sin." Outwardly "in the skin he is black, but not within" (*Sermon* 28:2).

We cannot doubt that Bernard falls within the Catholic tradition that recognizes that Jesus took upon himself the humanity of the fallen race of Adam. Equally, Bernard grasped that only in assuming our sinful flesh was Jesus able to restore it to its purity. Cf. *In Vigiliam Nativitatis,* Sermon 4.

[18]See *Summa Contra Gentiles,* IV,29-31. Translation from *On the Truth of the Catholic Faith,* eds. H. Anderson, A. Pegis, V.J. Bourke, and J. O'Neil (Garden City, NY: Image Books, 1955-1957). See also, *Summa Theologica,* III,5.

First, because it would seem to belong to justice that he who sinned should make amends; and hence that from the nature which he had corrupted should be assumed that whereby satisfaction was to be made for the whole nature. Secondly, it pertains to man's greater dignity that the conqueror of the devil should spring from the stock conquered by the devil. Thirdly, because God's power is thereby made more manifest since, from a corrupt and weakened nature, he assumed that which was raised to such might and glory.[19]

Firstly, Aquinas invariably gave priority to the soteriological significance of Jesus' "fallen" humanity. He recognized, along with Anselm, that if degenerate humanity were to be saved then one like us, while remaining sinless, ought to offer proper satisfaction to the Father:

But the penalty consequent on the sin of the human race is death and the other capacities for suffering of the present life. . . . Hence, the Apostle says: "By one man sin entered this world and by sin death" (Romans 5:12). Therefore, God had to assume without sin flesh capable of suffering and death, so that by suffering and dying he would satisfy for us and take away sin. And this is what the Apostle says, that "God sent his own Son in the likeness of sinful flesh" (Romans 8:3), that is, having flesh like that of sinners, namely, capable of suffering and death; and the Apostle adds "that of sin he might condemn sin in the flesh," that is, in order that by the penalty which he sustained in the flesh for our sin he might take sin away from us.[20]

[19] S.T., III,4,6. See also S.C.G., IV,30,28.
[20] S.C.G., IV,55,14.

Secondly, one who shouldered our human condition that sin impaired restored our human dignity and, yet, as one of us, he vanquished the lies and assaults of Satan while remaining obedient and loyal to the Father.

Lastly, since Jesus was vulnerable to temptation, suffering, and death, God's power is manifested the more in that he was ever faithful and thus raised to the highest glory.

Responding to the objection that for Jesus to assume a humanity from the lineage of Adam would make him a common sinner, Aquinas answered:

> Christ ought to be separated from sinners as regards sin, which he came to overthrow, and not as regards nature which he came to save, and in which "it behooved him in all things to be made like to his brethren," as the Apostle says (Hebrews 2:17). And in this is his innocence the more wonderful, seeing that though assumed from a mass tainted by sin, his nature was endowed with such purity.[21]

Aquinas here made an important distinction. The Son assumed a humanity that sin tainted, but did not assume original sin and he did not sin himself.[22] Thus Jesus did not inherit interior moral concupiscence or the "fomes" of sin.[23]

Freely Assumed Our Penalty

Aquinas then, along with Anselm and the patristic tradition, maintained that Jesus was free from the moral corruption of

---

[21] S.T., III,4,6, ad.1.

[22] Because the Holy Spirit conceived Jesus, "Christ did not receive human nature from Adam actively, but only materially—and from the Holy Spirit actively. . . . And thus Christ did not sin in Adam, in whom he was only as regards his matter" (ibid., III,15,1, ad. 2. See also, ad.3 & 4). See also, S.C.G., 52,9.

[23] See ibid., III,15,2.

original sin inherited from Adam's transgression. But, unlike Anselm, Aquinas recognized that to assume sinful flesh necessarily entailed assuming the penalty of sufferings that accrued to it. "His [flesh] was similar to 'sinful flesh,' for his was the captive of suffering, and such did the flesh of man become through sin."[24] It likewise was fitting for "God to assume a nature created, mutable, corporeal, and subject to penalty, but it did not become him to assume the evil of the fault."[25] Thus, Jesus suffered such penalties of sin as "hunger, thirst, death, and the like, which we suffer sensibly in this life [which] flow from original sin. And hence Christ, in order to satisfy fully for original sin, wished to suffer sensible pain, that he might consume death and the like in himself."[26] Was Jesus then necessarily subject to such human defects? "The Apostle says (Romans 8:3) that God sent 'his own Son in the likeness of sinful flesh.' Now it is a condition of sinful flesh to be under the necessity of dying, and suffering other like passions. Therefore the necessity of suffering these defects was in Christ's flesh."[27]

Nonetheless, Aquinas argued that just as Jesus assumed a nature without sin, so he could have assumed a nature without the penalties and defects of sin. Yet he chose to assume the defects and penalties of sin, not by way of necessary contraction, but by free choice: "Christ was made like to other men in the quality and not in the cause of these defects; and hence, unlike others, he did not contract them."[28] Aquinas here wished to assure a two-fold truth. He wanted to uphold

---

[24] *S.C.G.,* IV,29,7. Aquinas affirmed that Jesus' humanity was truly passable and that he could experience pain, sorrow, fear, wonder, and anger. See *S.T.,* III,15,4-9.

[25] *S.T.,* III,1,1, ad.3.

[26] *Ibid.,* III,1,4, ad. 2. Cf. III,5,2, ad.2. Aquinas consistently places the assumption of the defects of sin within a soteriological context. Cf. III,15,4.

[27] *Ibid.,* III,14,2.

[28] *Ibid.,* III,14,3, ad.3. Cf. III,14,3, and ad.1.

Christ's sinlessness and thus the absence of any interior, personal, or moral necessity that he assume our penalties. In other words, Christ was not born morally corrupted by sin and thus deserving and acquiring the just penalties of sin. Equally, Aquinas maintained that the quality and extent of Jesus' penalties and sufferings were the same as for those whom sin morally corrupted, and who thus deserved condemnation. Contrary to Anselm, Aquinas confirmed that while Jesus was preserved from the moral defects of sin, nonetheless the sufferings and penalties of sin flowed directly from his freely assuming the humanity of Adam's race, and not from something he freely assumed and acquired in addition to his humanity: "Thus it is clear that Christ did not contract these defects as if taking them upon himself as due to sin, but by his own will."[29]

Aquinas was unwaveringly faithful to his perception that Jesus' humanity bore the birthmark of sin. For example, Aquinas answered affirmatively the question of whether it was fitting for Jesus to have been baptized. By his baptism, Jesus not only purified and sanctified the waters of sacramental baptism, but he also (quoting Chrysostom) testified, having assumed a "sinful nature," one in the "likeness to sinful flesh," that such a carnal nature was in need of baptism.[30] Moreover, for Aquinas, Jesus had so profoundly woven himself into the sinful fabric of humanity that he descended into hell:

He came to bear our penalty in order to free us from penalty. ... But through sin man had incurred not only death of the body, but also descent into hell. Consequently since it was fitting for Christ to die in order to deliver us from death, so

---

[29] *Ibid.*, III,14,3. Cf. *ibid.*, ad.1.
[30] *Ibid.*, III,39,1. Cf. John Chrysostom, *Homilia 4 in Matthaeum.*

it was fitting for him to descend into hell in order to deliver us also from going down into hell.[31]

Despite Aquinas' clear teaching that, in the Incarnation, the eternal Son assumed Adam's sinful flesh and thus truly became one of us, subsequent Christology did not perceive its significance or develop his arguments and advance his judgments. Rather the christological tradition fostered and elevated, sometimes to extremes, other converse aspects of Aquinas' teaching, such as Jesus' sinlessness and holiness, or that he always possessed the beatific vision and enjoyed infused knowledge which expelled ignorance.[32] In the process, the christological tradition lost sight of the historical Jesus in a cloud of theological speculation and, with this loss, the depth of the New Testament proclamation. This study wishes to recover and

---

[31] *Ibid.*, III,52,1. Cf. III,52,4. However, we should note that Aquinas held that Jesus descended into that hell where only the just were detained and not into the hell of the lost. Nonetheless this was an experience of separation from God. Cf. *ibid.*, III,52,2.

[32] Cf. *ibid.*, III,2,12; III,7,1-2 & 9; III,9,2-3; III,10; III,11; III,15,3.

For brief accounts of these later developments, see *The New Catholic Encylopedia*, Vol. 7 (New York: McGraw-Hill, 1966), 937-39. See also *Dictionnaire de Théologie Catholique*, Vol. 8 (Paris: Librarie Letouzey et Ane, 1924), col. 1271-74.

For a mature expression of these developments, see Bernard Lonergan, *De Verbo Incarnato* (Romae: Pontificia Universitas Gregoriana, 1964), theses 11-15.

Alexis Cardinal Lepicier (1863-1936) in his *Institutiones Theologicae Dogmaticae ad Texum S. Thomae Concinnatae* held that Jesus knew all mathematics, science, languages, etc.

The Catholic Church has defined that Jesus was sinless and did not suffer the effects of sin, specifically concupiscence. Cf. Denzinger-Schonmetzer, Second Council of Constantinople (A.D. 553), 434; the Lateran Council (A.D. 649), 505; the Eleventh Council of Toledo (A.D. 675), 539.

advance these forgotten Thomistic insights, and to do so by exploiting, beyond perhaps Aquinas, the rich biblical testimony.

CHAPTER FIVE

JESUS' HUMANITY:
CONTEMPORARY CHRISTOLOGY

In the last one hundred and fifty years, there have been several theologians, Edward Irving, Karl Barth, and Hans Urs von Balthasar, who have creatively taken up the topic of our study—Jesus' sinful flesh. We will study them below. However, on the whole, our subject, for a number of reasons, has not attracted great attention.

Firstly, this lack of attention is due historically both to its almost entire neglect since the middle ages and also to the current christological emphasis, rooted in the nineteenth century, concerning the psychology or inner subjectivity of the human Jesus. Today's questions focus on issues such as: Did Jesus humanly know who he was? What awareness did he have of his ministry? What was his subjective experience of the Father? Whether and how was his divine consciousness compatible with his human consciousness and vice versa? How are we to understand the divine personhood of Jesus (as the Councils proclaimed) in relationship to his human subjective personality (as featured in contemporary philosophy and psychology)?

Secondly, with this contemporary accent on the human subjectivity of Jesus and the often subsequent de-emphasis of his divine personhood, there has been, paradoxically, a defensive emphasis on the man Jesus' union or relationship with God/Son/Word so as not to be accused of some heresy, such as adoptionism.[1]

---

[1] For examples and analysis of this type of Christology, see Chapter One, footnote 4.

Despite the original intent, this tactical maneuver has shifted the christological focus to a demonstration of how the man Jesus significantly differed from us (and thus was in some manner uniquely divine). To emphasize within this christological framework how and why Jesus was in the likeness of sinful flesh would add only another unwanted conundrum. How can the man Jesus be in the likeness of sinful flesh and yet, as man, still provide some unique and definitive expression of his relationship to God?[2] The lesson to be learned is that whenever the divine personhood of Christ is not accorded its proper standing, his authentic humanity is consequently and immediately imperiled because it is then forced to bear the "divine" weight left in its absence.

Lastly, within our contemporary theological and christological milieu, there has been an obvious devaluation of sin (both original and personal) and our consequent alienation from God.[3] With this devaluation comes the diminishing need

---

[2] The historical harbinger of this type of Christology is F.D.E. Schleiermacher, *The Christian Faith*, trs. H.R. Mackintosh and J.S. Stewart (Edinburgh: T. & T. Clark, 1928). Schleiermacher denied the traditional notion of the Incarnation, that the eternal Son of God came to exist as a man. In its place, Schleiermacher substituted a Christology of God-consciousness. Jesus' divinity consisted in his human consciousness' being thoroughly centered upon and absorbed by the divine. Paradoxically, what happens in such a Christology is that, while it is proffered in order to make Jesus more like us, in actual fact, it makes him less like us for it makes his humanity so radically different from our own. There could have been no inner conflict, no true agony or struggle. The historical, concrete, human Jesus, with his temptations and sufferings, would have been absorbed in the Buddha- or Hindu-like mystical and ethereal clouds of divine consciousness.

[3] The view that original sin is not so much a deficiency within the individual person, but rather an expression of residual imperfection remaining within the evolutionary process or of the sinfulness inherent within human social structures and systems exemplifies this trend. In such a setting, personal sin is seen not so much as something evil that a person

for this now "not-so-sinful" man to make appropriate reparation, atonement, and expiation to the all-loving God. In
addition, humankind has no need for radical re-creation.
Thus, the soteriological basis for Jesus' being of our sinful stock
is withdrawn. Since we are okay, so too is he.

In contrast to the above, both Barth and von Balthasar have
firmly upheld the traditional view of the Incarnation, having
taken seriously the sinful state of humanity in all its ramifications, and in turn professed the necessity that sacrificial
reparation be made to God. They are equally the ones who
have creatively grasped the significance of Jesus' taking upon
himself a humanity that sin has tarnished. All of these truths
form the one grand mosaic of redemption.

Protestant Christology: Edward Irving

In his *Church Dogmatics*, Karl Barth (1886-1968) discussed
the question of our study. However, before examining his
position, we should by way of setting the historical context
study briefly someone of the Protestant Reformed tradition

freely wills to do, but merely as an acknowledgment that a person is
immersed in a still imperfect social, cultural, and political milieu. In
response to this understanding of sin, Pope John Paul II has written: "There
is one meaning sometimes given to *social sin* that is not legitimate or
acceptable, even though it is very common in certain quarters today. This
usage contrasts *social sin* and *personal sin,* not without ambiguity, in a way
that leads more or less unconsciously to the watering down and almost the
abolition of *personal sin,* with the recognition only of *social* guilt and
responsibilities. . . . Practically every sin is a social sin, in the sense that
blame for it is to be placed not so much on the moral conscience of an
individual but rather on some vague entity or anonymous collectivity, such
as the situation, the system, society, structures, or institutions." *Reconciliatio
et Paenitentia (On Reconciliation and Penance)* (Boston: St. Paul Editions,
1984), 16. See also Sacred Congregation for the Doctrine of the Faith,
Instruction on Certain Aspects of the "Theology of Liberation"(1984), IV, 14-
15.

(with its customary emphasis on our sinful condition) to whom Barth refers favorably—the Scottish theologian, Edward Irving (1792-1834).[4]

Irving was a popular and often controversial preacher. He was excommunicated from the Church of Scotland for his work, *The Orthodox and Catholic Doctrine of our Lord's Human Nature.* While not the actual founder, he was closely associated with the origins of the "Catholic Apostolic Church." The "Irvingites," as the adherents of this denomination were sometimes called, expected the immanent Second Coming of Jesus. Irving's association with this unconventional revival further undermined his ecclesial and theological standing, and so contributed to the view that his Christology was but another example of his religious eccentricity.[5]

While Irving fervently professed a Chalcedonian Christology, he also equally taught that Jesus assumed a sinful humanity: "That Christ took our fallen nature is most manifest, because there is no other in existence to take."[6] When Jesus became man, he "submitted himself to the very condition of a sinner."[7] He took on the "substance of fallen Adam:"[8]

In that act of incarnation we behold the nature of sinful, fallen, suffering man entering into sweet and harmonious

---

[4] See Karl Barth, *Church Dogmatics*, I.2, trs. G.T. Thomson and Harold Knight (Edinburgh: T. & T. Clark, 1956), 154.

[5] For an excellent study of Irving's Christology placed within the historical context of his life and times, see Gordon Strachan, *The Pentecostal Theology of Edward Irving* (Peabody, Ma: Hendrickson Publishers, 1973).

[6] Edward Irving, *The Collected Writings of Edward Irving in Five Volumes*, Vol. 5, ed. G. Carlyle (London: Alexander Strachan, 1865), 115. For an excellent article on Irving's Christology, see Colin Gunton, "Two Dogmas Revisited: Edward Irving's Christology," *The Scottish Journal of Theology* 41 (1988): 366ff. We are greatly indebted to Gunton's work.

[7] *Ibid.*, 28.

[8] *Ibid.*, 59.

union with the sinless nature of God. . .the most violent of all contradictions reconciled; and a door of hope, yea, and of assurance, opened, which no power shall ever shut.[9]

Irving was condemned for espousing this sinful humanity of Jesus.[10]

Irving argued, reminiscent of the early Fathers, that only if Jesus took upon himself sinful flesh could sinful flesh be saved: "If Christ took upon himself our fallen and corruptible nature, and brought it through death into eternal glory, then is the act of the will of Christ not to lay down, but to assume or take up humanity into himself."[11] It is in and through our fallen nature that the Son of God defeated sin and all of the temptations of the Evil One: "His flesh is the fit field of contention because it is the same on which Satan had triumphed since the fall. Here, then, in the flesh of Christ, is the great controversy waged." While Jesus' flesh was "linked to all material things, devil-possessed," yet his soul, through the Spirit within him, was set on the will of God.[12] For Irving:

If Christ took not our substance in its fallen, but in its unfallen state, and brought this unto glory, then nothing whatever hath been proved with respect to fallen creatures, such as we are. The work of Christ is to toucheth not us who are fallen; there is not reconciliation of the fallen creature unto God; God is not in Christ reconciling a sinful world, but he is in Christ reconciling an unfallen world; for it is the

[9] *Ibid* 327-28.
[10] For the history of this controversy, as well as an examination of Irving's Christology, see Strachan, 25-52.
[11] *Ibid.*, 148. Cf. 213.
[12] *Ibid.*, 161.

unfallen creature and the Godhead which have met in Christ.[13]

Nonetheless for Irving, Jesus did not actually sin, which is to his great merit for he lived as one of us within our sinful humanity.[14] Only by living a sinless life in sinful flesh could Jesus transform it and make it holy: "This is truly the work of God, which was wrought in and upon the human nature of Jesus Christ, to bring a clean thing out of an unclean, and to begin the work of regeneration in the fallen world."[15]

We can see Irving's true importance as well in the proper place he gives to the Holy Spirit within the Incarnation. Here, Irving advances the tradition for rarely has Christology accorded the Holy Spirit such a prominent position.

While truly the eternal Son of God became man, nonetheless, since he assumed a human nature of the sinful race of Adam, he must, as must all of mankind, live by the Spirit. Irving believed that to rely solely on the Son's divinity as the solitary source of holiness within the humanity of Jesus bordered on Docetism or Monophysitism:[16]

Be it known unto these gainsayers, that in Christ, and in the soul redeemed by Christ, and in the world redeemed by Christ, we can do as ill without the divinity of the Holy Ghost as we can without the divinity of the Son. We have

[13] *Ibid.,* 158; cf. 141, 144-46, 565.
[14] See *ibid.,* 4-5, 36-37, 137, 141.
[15] *Ibid.,* 145. Cf. 148, 565.
[16] See *ibid.,* 123-24. We can see the authenticity of Irving's Christology in his belief that it is wrong to attribute some actions of Christ to his divinity (miracles) and others to his humanity (eating). Rather, within the Incarnation, it is always the Son of God acting as man "through the mighty power of the Holy Ghost" (p. 134).

a fallen world to redeem, we have the Son of God to redeem it: but these two must not intermingle or be confused with each other; and therefore, in order to make that fallen creature harmonious with the Godhead of the Son, and so to obtain one person, we must have in it the life of the Holy Ghost, overcoming the death of sin.[17]

Throughout the life of Jesus, from conception to resurrection, the Holy Spirit was thus necessarily active: "The Holy Ghost was the author of his bodily life, the quickener of that substance which he took from fallen humanity."[18] Because Jesus was as we are, he was "liable to all the temptations to which flesh is liable: but the soul of Christ, thus anointed with the Holy Ghost, did ever resist and reject the suggestions of evil."[19] He was "liable to all temptation, that through it he might be tempted like as we are; but that his temptations through its union to his body, as my soul is to my body united, was yet, through its having been taken possession of by the holy Ghost. . .prevented from ever yielding to any of those temptations."[20] "The flesh of Christ was the middle space on which the powers of the world contended with the Holy Spirit dwelling in his soul."[21] As all had fallen in Adam, so all were subsumed and renewed in the humanity of Jesus: "Christ's life from his baptism to his agony is our model of the liberty and power of the Holy Ghost."[22]

---

[17] *Ibid.,* 169-70.

[18] *Ibid.,* 126.

[19] *Ibid.*

[20] *Ibid.,* 128.

[21] *Ibid.,* 161. Cf. 162-71.

[22] *Ibid.,* 237. Cf. 233-46, 320-21, 564. Strachan argues, quite convincingly, that there is a close relationship between Irving's Christology and his pentecostal theology concerning Baptism in the Spirit and the gifts of the Spirit. Our radical new life in the Holy Spirit with the manifestation of the

Irving defended his position by appealing to reality.[23] Sin was and is a reality. Our separation from God was and is a reality. The feebleness of our flesh was and is a reality. Our salvation must be equally as real. Irving believed that only if Jesus confronted this reality in his own frail humanity could he heal and transform our depraved humanity. Only through the assuming of sinful flesh could he, in reality, restore us to God.

Protestant Christology: Karl Barth

Barth did not shun Irving's assessment of the Incarnation, but staunchly confirmed its validity within his own Christology.[24]

---

spiritual gifts, enumerated in 1 Cor 12 is the direct result of Jesus' having assumed our sinful humanity and radically transforming it in and through his death and resurrection. Christians now share in the new humanity of Christ with the full power and life of the Holy Spirit. See 87-147.

[23] See *ibid.*, 566.

[24] For Barth's assessment of Irving as well as of Calvin and other Protestants on this issue, see *Church Dogmatics*, I.2, 152-55.

Barth in these pages quotes other Protestant theologians who have argued for a similar position. For example: Gottfried Menken (1812) wrote: "The Son of God when he came into the world did not then assume a human nature such as this nature was when it came forth from God's hand, before the Fall. . . . On the contrary, it was a human nature such as was in Adam after the Fall and is in all his successors" (*Homilie ub Hebr. 9:13*, Works, Vol. 3, p. 332). Or J.C.K. von Hofmann stated: Jesus "desired his human nature to be the means of manifesting his personal communion with God, but manifesting it within human nature as limited and conditioned by sin" (*Der Schriftbeweis*, I, 1852, p. 45). Edward Bohl wrote: "The Logos entered our condition thus alienated from God, or the nature which sinned. But our condition is that through Adam we have passed into guiltiness and become liable to death, in consequence of which we are enemies of God and hated by him. . . . Either the Son of God brings salvation to pass under conditions of life like ours or else everyone has to start all over again and to fulfill independently God's claim upon us" (*Dogmatik*, 1887, pp. 209, 302).

In so doing, Barth desired to revive an authentic and, along with Irving, true-to-life evangelical Christology.

For Barth, so great is God's love that in becoming flesh he "puts himself on the side of his own adversary:"

> What the New Testament calls *sarx* includes not only the concept of man in general but also. . .the narrower concept of the man who is liable to the judgment and verdict of God, who having become incapable of knowing and loving God must incur the wrath of God, whose existence has become one exposed to death because he has sinned against God. Flesh is the concrete form of human nature marked by Adam's fall, the concrete form of that entire world which, when seen in the light of Christ's death on the cross, must be regarded as the old world already past and gone, the form of the destroyed nature and existence of man as they have to be reconciled with God.[25]

Barth did not deny that Jesus was holy, innocent, and with-out sin: "He was not a sinful man." Yet for Barth, this is truly significant only insofar as Jesus lived this holy and righteous life within the confines of a humanity marked by Adam's fall. Jesus, for Barth, must be like us if he is to have any significant impact on our condition:

> Inwardly and outwardly his situation was that of a sinful man. He did nothing that Adam did. But he lived a life in the form it must take on the basis and assumption of Adam's act. He bore innocently what Adam and all of us in Adam have been guilty of. . . . There must be no weakening or obscuring of the saving truth that the nature which God assumed in Christ is identical with our nature as we see it in

[25] *Ibid.*, 151.

the light of the Fall. If it were otherwise, how could Christ be really like us?[26]

Echoing the now classical soteriological concerns, Barth recognized that our reconciliation with God and the transformation of our own humanity were dependent upon Jesus' drawing near to us and, as one of us, doing in our sinful flesh what we ourselves could not do—being obedient and loyal to the Father:

> That is, in the likeness of sinful flesh (unholy flesh, marked by sin), there happens the unlike, the new and helpful thing, that sin is condemned by not being committed, by being omitted, by full obedience now being found in the very place where otherwise sin necessarily and irresistibly takes place. The meaning of the incarnation is that now in the flesh that is not done what all flesh does.[27]

This means that Jesus experienced the effects of sin within his own humanity and yet did not sin:

> The point is that, faced with God, Jesus did not run away from the state and situation of fallen man, but took it upon himself, lived it and bore it himself as the eternal Son of God. How could he have done so, if in his human existence he had not been exposed to real inward temptation and trial, if like other men he had not trodden an inner path, if he had not cried to God and wrestled with God in real inward need? It was in this wrestling, in which he was in solidarity with us to the uttermost, that there was done that which is not done in us, the will of God.[28]

---

[26] *Ibid.*, 152-53.
[27] *Ibid.*, 156.
[28] *Ibid.*, 158.

Barth professed that the Word's becoming flesh was God's greatest condescension—"this consummation of God's condescension, this inconceivability which is greater than the inconceivability of the divine majesty and the inconceivability of human darkness put together."[29]

Protestantism, not without cause, has often been criticized for its view that sin has utterly and thoroughly corrupted human nature. This extreme is seen in the anthropology and predestinationism of Calvin, as well as in the doctrine of forensic justification of Luther (and more so in his followers, such as Oecolampadius). Nonetheless, the more moderate form of this tradition maintained the true seriousness of sin, and thus preserved, as Irving (despite his excommunication) and Barth testified, in a way that Catholic post-Tridentine Christology did not, the necessity that Jesus be born of the stock of Adam if on the cross he was to reconcile us to the just and loving God and thus heal our humanity.

Catholic Cristology: Hans Urs von Balthasar

We have noted already that the Catholic Manual Theology of the nineteenth and twentieth centuries championed the perfection of Jesus' humanity and did not further the insights of many of the Fathers and of Anselm and Aquinas who advocated a humanity defiled by sin. However, the truth that Jesus lived a human life marred by sin did not completely vanish. For example, even John Henry Cardinal Newman (1801-1890) who, in reaction to the liberal anti-dogmatism of his day, underscored the doctrine that Jesus was truly God, nonetheless, through his study of the patristic tradition, came to esteem the humanity of Jesus.

[29] Ibid., 152.

Reflecting the heritage we have seen develop, Newman preached that the only-begotten Son of God became thoroughly as we are, yet without sin:

> He, indeed, when man fell, might have remained in the glory which he had with the Father before the world was. But that unsearchable Love, which showed itself in our original creation, rested not content with a frustrated work, but brought him down again from his Father's bosom to do his will, and repair the evil which sin had caused. And with a wonderful condescension he came, not as before in power, but in weakness, in the form of a servant, in the likeness of that fallen creature whom he purposed to restore. So he humbled himself; suffering all the infirmities of our nature in the likeness of sinful flesh, all but a sinner,—pure from all sin, yet subjected to all temptation,—and at length becoming obedient unto death, even the death of the cross.[30]

Similarly in his hymn "Praise to the Holiest," Newman referred to Jesus as a "second Adam" who "to our rescue came."

Newman's testimony bears witness that while the perfect humanity of Jesus may have prevailed within academic theology, within Catholic devotion and piety, it was the humble and lowly Jesus in the likeness of sinful flesh who still moved the hearts and minds of the faithful. Fittingly, this embodies the motto Newman chose on his elevation as Cardinal: *Cor ad cor loquitur.*

Hans Urs von Balthasar (1905-1988) possessed a keen perception of Jesus' sinful humanity and so retrieved the Catholic heritage. Or, in the alternative, he acquired a clearer

---

[30] John Henry Newman, "Sermon 3: The Incarnation," *Parochial and Plain Sermons,* II (San Francisco: Ignatius Press, 1987), 244-45.

understanding of Jesus' enfeebled human condition by attempting to reclaim the full Catholic tradition. Either way, he sought to embrace without apology all the ramifications of this mystery. In so doing, he confirmed that this truth is the inherent and indispensable christological prolegomenon to soteriology.

For von Balthasar, Jesus' sinful humanity provided the essential and vital bond between the Incarnation and the cross. The seizing of the humanity bearing Adam's birthmark thrust the eternal Son directly to the cross: "To 'take on manhood' means in fact to assume its concrete destiny with all that entails—suffering, death, hell—in solidarity with every human being."[31] Thus "he who says Incarnation, also says Cross."[32] The reason is simple and clear—the Son assumed a humanity afflicted by sin and thus must have inherited the penalty of that condition—death and judgment: "The Son of God took a human nature in its fallen condition, and with it, therefore, the worm in its entrails—mortality, fallenness, self-estrangement, death—which sin introduced into the world."[33]

Having entered into our sinful condition and having embraced our sin, Jesus experienced the full weight of sin's judgment and condemnation. In the Garden of Olives, Jesus suffered the horror of so great a burden:[34] "Since the sin of the world is 'laid' upon him, Jesus no longer distinguishes himself

---

[31] Hans Urs von Balthasar, *Mysterium Paschale,* tr. A. Nichols, O.P. (Edinburgh: T. & T. Clark, 1990), 20. See the entire first chapter (pp. 11-48) for von Balthasar's complete account of how the Incarnation directly leads to the passion.

[32] *Ibid.,* 22.

[33] *Ibid.* See also *The Von Balthasar Reader,* eds. M. Kehl and W. Loser, trs. R. Daly and F. Lawrence (New York: Crossroad, 1982), 144-45, 148, 150.

[34] See *ibid.,* 100-107. See also *The Von Balthasar Reader,* 147-48.

and his fate from those of sinners. . .and thus in that way he experiences the anxiety and horror which they by rights should have known for themselves."[35] On the cross, Jesus died in the place of humankind and, as "a sinner," died on the cross freeing everyone from the curse of sin.[36]

To look upon the cross of Christ is to see God's judgment of sin:

> Above all, the Cross is the full achievement of the divine judgment on "sin" (2 Corinthians 5:21) summed up, dragged into the daylight and suffered through in the Son. Moreover, the sending of the Son in "sinful flesh" took place only so as to make it possible to "condemn (*katakrinein*) sin in the flesh" (Romans 8:2).[37]

We observe here one of von Balthasar's chief emphases: the substitutionary nature of Jesus' sacrifice. Jesus assumed our condition; he stood in our stead. In perfect obedience and love for us and the Father, he endured the curse of sin, our condemnation, and so liberated us from experiencing so grave a judgment.[38]

Jesus' lifeless corpse is then the most convincing testimony that he inherited his humanity from Adam: "Jesus was really dead, because he really became a man as we are, a son of Adam."[39] Pressing the point to its ultimate conclusion, von Balthasar appropriates the ancient, patristic, soteriological principle and asserts that Jesus, in order to heal the dead, was

---

[35] *Ibid.*, 104. See 105.

[36] *Ibid.*, 134.

[37] *Ibid.*, 119. For von Balthasar, the cross of Jesus tells us that "God hates sin" (*ibid.*, 138).

[38] See *ibid.*, 134-36.

[39] *Ibid.*, 148.

in solidarity with the dead. He, like them, was passive, helpless and lifeless.[40]

Moreover, drawing upon the Holy Saturday experience of his spiritual intimate, Adrienne von Speyr, von Balthasar accentuates the truth that Jesus, in accordance with his fallen condition, underwent both the abandonment of God and the condemnation of hell. Aligning himself with Aquinas who concluded that Jesus descended into hell precisely because he had assumed our sinful nature, von Balthasar judges that it is here that Jesus endured the complete and outright actuality of our sin—the utter helplessness and terror of being separated from God and the absolute inability to rectify the situation. As one of us, Jesus experienced the *poena damni*, the second death: "Jesus does not only accept the (to be sure, accursed) mortal destiny of Adam. He also, quite expressly, carries the sin of the human race and, with those sins, the 'second death' of God-abandonment."[41]

On Holy Saturday there is the descent of the dead Jesus to hell, that is (put very simply) his solidarity in the period of nontime with those who have lost their way from God. Their choice—with which they have chosen to put their I in place of God's selfless love—is definitive. Into this finality (of death) the dead Son descends, no longer acting in any way, but stripped by the cross of every power and initiative of his own, as one purely to be used, debased to mere matter, with a fully indifferent (corpse) obedience, incapable of any active act of solidarity—only thus is he right for any 'sermon' to the dead.[42]

[40] See *ibid.*, 160-65.
[41] *Ibid.*, 90. See *ibid.*, 148-88.
[42] *The Von Balthasar Reader*, 153.

Now lying abandoned and tormented in the depths of hell, Jesus, according to von Balthasar, manifests the magnitude of God's love. So great is the Father's love that he would "hand over" his Son to such a fate and so great is the Son's love that he would so endure it.[43] His cry from the cross expressed a horrific truth and yet one that is for us a lasting hope: "My God, my God, why have you forsaken me?" (Mk 15:34). We need no longer fear death with its condemnation, for Jesus, on our behalf and in our place, entered into our death and preserved us from everlasting abandonment.[44] Such love, fidelity, and obedience merited for us forgiveness and recon-ciliation and, for himself, exaltation at the Father's right hand.

Despite this brief summary of von Balthasar's thought, we can see clearly how critical is the sinful humanity of Jesus for his Christology and soteriology. Only if Jesus had assumed our fallen nature and, with it, our sin and condemnation could he endure our punishment and embrace our sentence. Having done so in faithful obedience to the Father and in love for us, he not only freed us, who now live a new life in him, from such a destiny, but he likewise reconciled us to the Father so as to share in the present and future glory of his resurrected body.[45]

Thus, von Balthasar has reclaimed and furthered a biblical, realistic understanding of sin and its effects— alienation from God and abandonment in hell—and with this authenticity, an equally genuine and graphic appreciation of Jesus' historical humanity sculptured by the Fall. He has, in turn, given new

---

[43] See *Mysterium Paschale*, 107-12.

[44] See *ibid.*, 167-68.

[45] See *ibid.* the whole of chapter 5, "Going to the Father, Easter," 189-280. For another brief but excellent summary of van Balthasar's thought on the pascal mystery, see John O'Donnell, *The Mystery of the Triune God* (New York: Paulist Press, 1989), 60-72.

credibility, relevance, and gravity to Jesus as our substitute within Catholic soteriology.

****

Our historical survey has gained for us three significant conclusions:

1. The christological tradition definitively confirms that the eternal Son assumed a humanity which bore the birthmark of Adam. He became man in the likeness of sinful flesh;
2. This truth is of irrefutable soteriological significance. Only if Jesus became as we are, defiled by sin, could he, on our behalf, freely assume our condemnation and lovingly offer (in the Spirit) his holy and innocent life to the Father in reparation for our sin; and
3. In so becoming a son of Adam, Jesus through his cross and resurrection healed our humanity so that we can now become a new creation in him. Invariably and without deviation, the governing tenet is: what is not assumed (in its entirety) is not saved.

PART THREE:

JESUS' SINFUL HUMANITY IN THE NEW TESTAMENT

We have come now to the heart of our inquiry. What does the New Testament tell us about the humanity of Jesus? Specifically, does it profess that Jesus was born of the sinful race of Adam, and does it understand this to be essential to our salvation? We hope to show that the New Testament not only affirms that Jesus participated in our sinful human condition, but also attests to how vital this is.

Addressing our thesis from a New Testament perspective, we can have two possible approaches. The first is to examine the Incarnation and then proceed to study the events of Jesus' life (baptism, temptations, transfiguration, etc.) culminating with his death and resurrection. This approach is chronological. However, we prefer a second approach, one that follows the order of faith and knowledge.

Reflecting on this order of faith and knowledge, contemporary scholars almost universally agree that the New Testament communities and authors interpreted Jesus' birth and life in light of his cross and resurrection. They fully appreciated the significance of the Son's assuming our humanity only in light of what he accomplished as man, through his death and resurrection. They also appreciated how, through faith, these paschal events changed their lives. The cross and resurrection became then the principal hermeneutic for interpreting Jesus'

Incarnation, baptism, temptations, etc. These in turn shed further light on the cross and resurrection, thus closing the hermeneutical circle.

We will begin our study of the humanity of Jesus by examining some aspects of Pauline soteriology. While Paul's theology bears his own personal stamp and emphasis, yet because he is the earliest New Testament author, he provides us with a starting point.

CHAPTER SIX

ST. PAUL: "HE BECAME SIN FOR US"

Paul envisaged Jesus almost exclusively as risen and glorious—as the heavenly Lord. Jesus' historical acts and words, except for his passion and death, rarely appear in Paul's letters (cf. 1 Cor 1:20-31; 11:23-26; Gal 4:4-5). We must not conclude, however, that the human, earthly Jesus was of no importance to Paul. Rather, Jesus' historical humanity was indispensable to Paul's soteriology.

Dying and Rising in Christ

Paul grew in his understanding of the content of faith not through mere speculation, but from his lived experience—what had happened to him and his fellow converts upon and subsequent to their conversion. The interior, transforming power of the Spirit became for Paul an interpretive tool for comprehending the significance of the earthly, human Jesus—of the Incarnation—and of what he had accomplished: the work of the cross and the new life of the Resurrection. This is important for we contend that Jesus' human actions are of the utmost relevance because they embody meaning and bring about change.

Romans 6 (and, as we will see, other passages as well) clearly illustrates this point. Paul's experience of Christian baptism allowed him to discern the implications of the Incarnation and to plumb the depths of the cross and resurrection.

Having stated that where sin abounds, grace abounds even more, Paul assured the Romans that they should not therefore continue sinning:

How can we who died to sin still live in it? Do you not know that all of us who have been baptized into Christ Jesus were baptized into his death? We were buried therefore with him by baptism into death, so that as Christ was raised from the dead by the glory of the Father, we too might walk in newness of life. For if we have been united with him in a death like his, we shall certainly be united with him in a resurrection like his. We know that our old self was crucified with him so that the sinful body might be destroyed, and we might no longer be enslaved to sin. For he who has died is freed from sin. But if we have died with Christ, we believe that we shall also live with him. For we know that Christ being raised from the dead will never die again; death no longer has dominion over him. The death he died he died to sin, once for all, but the life he lives he lives to God. So you also must consider yourselves dead to sin and alive to God in Christ Jesus. (Rom 6:2-11).

The good news of Jesus Christ is that through faith and baptism, we are radically transformed. Christians "die to sin." We "walk in newness of life." Our transformation is a participation in the same transformation Jesus himself underwent. We are "baptized into his death." Christians are not, through baptism, merely affiliated figuratively or symbolically to the death of Christ. Rather, for Paul, we are actually inserted into his very act of dying. Moreover, we are "buried with him," that is, we are literally "co-buried" (*synthaptein*) with him; together, we share the same grave. Thus, we also share in his Resurrection. As Christ now shares in the glory of the Father so, too, do we who have died with him. In this light, we walk in the newness of life.[1]

---

[1] See J. Fitzmyer, *The New Jerome Biblical Commentary,* eds. R. Brown, J. Fitzmyer, R.E. Murphy (Englewood Cliffs: Prentice Hall, 1990), 847.

Our re-creation is possible only because our "old self" (*palaios hemon anthropos*), that is, for Paul, our corrupted humanity enslaved by ungodly passions and drives, was crucified with Christ. Thus our "sinful body" (literally, "body of sin," *to soma tes hamartias*) which, for Paul, is not our material body as opposed to our soul, but the whole person mastered by the disposition of sin, was destroyed. But how could our "old self" compelled by sin die with Christ?

If our old self was crucified with Christ, as Paul proclaimed, then Jesus must have partaken of our sinful human condition. His humanity must have been of the sinful race of Adam. If Jesus did not possess a humanity scarred and tainted by sin, then our "old self" or "sinful body" did not die. Some other humanity may have died, but not one like our own. But that is precisely what Paul said must die and did die. Clearly, Paul predicated his theology of baptism upon the premise that Jesus, in the Incarnation, assumed a humanity like our own. Only then would "the death he died" be a death "to sin, once for all."

This conclusion is equally implied in Paul's declaration that because Jesus is now risen, "death no longer has dominion over him" (Rom 6:9). Paul assumed that death did reign over Jesus' earthly humanity. For Paul, this dominion is a direct consequence of sin: "Sin came into the world through one man and death through sin" (Rom 5:12). Thus, Jesus' death manifested his solidarity with our human sinful condition.

Moreover, our salvation is then the immediate result of the redemption of Jesus' own humanity. He was the first to have been delivered from the enslavement of the fallen human condition, for only after he died was he, and were we, in union with him through baptism, "freed from sin" (Rom 6:6-7; cf. 7:1-6).

A similar argument is found within the later Pauline tradition. The Letter to the Colossians compares baptism to circumcision: "In him also you were circumcised with a circumcision made without hands, by putting off the body of flesh in the circumcision of Christ; and you were buried with him in baptism, in which you were also raised with him through faith" (Col 2:11; cf. 2 Tim 2:11). To grasp the significance of this passage, we need to make two preliminary comments.

Firstly, the Pauline notion of flesh (*sarkos*) is similar to that of "the body of sin." "The flesh" connotes the whole person absorbed in complete self-centeredness and engrossed in the desires and passions of this earthly life.[2] *Sarx* breeds then the

[2] In some few cases, Paul uses *sarx* in a value-free manner, as designating merely the entire earthly, human being (see Gal 1:16; 2:20; 1 Cor 15:50; Rom 6:19). However, Paul normally sees human beings as either living in the flesh (*sarx*) or in the spirit (*pneuma*), that is, under the influence of God's Spirit and thus participating in the new eschatological reality of salvation (see Gal 3:3; 4:29; Rom 8:4-9,13). *Sarx* then specifies the person's opposition to the Spirit and the things of God (see 1 Cor 3:3; Phil 7:5; Rom 8:3). To be in the flesh is to live in sin and to suffer death as the consequence of sin (Rom 7:5; 8:13; 2 Cor 10:2). The fleshly mind is at enmity with God (see Rom 8:7). It follows the lusts of the flesh (see Gal 5:13,16). Thus those who live according to the flesh cannot please God (see Rom 8:8). The deeds of the flesh (bickering, rage, jealousy, lust, hatred, etc.) are enumerated in Gal 5:19-21. Kümmel summarizes Paul's notion of *sarx* by stating: "It characterizes the action of man who stands before God and instead of acknowledging God, trusts in himself. For Paul sees man always in a slave-master relationship, either to God or to sin. . . . Thus for Paul flesh is 'the mark of man as he is distinguished from God' and it characterizes man, not according to his existence, but according to his historical conduct in the world that is passing away." Werner Georg Kümmel, *The Theology of the New Testament* (Nashville: Abingdon, 1978), 178, cf. 174-78. See also Joseph Fitzmyer, *The New Jerome Biblical Commentary*, 1406-07; Gerhard Kittle, Gerhard Friedrich, eds., *Theological Dictionary of the New Testament*, Vol. VII (Grand Rapids: Eerdmans, 1971), 125-38. Unlike living in *sarx*, which enslaves man to the sin of this world, living in the *pneuma* is a sharing in the life with God. Christians no longer live in the flesh, sin, and death, but in the Spirit (Rom 8:2-4,12-13). They are concerned with the things of the Spirit (Rom 8:5) because the Spirit of God dwells in

corrupt drives within us that are the source of all sinful deeds (cf. Gal 5:19-21).

Secondly, in the Old Testament, circumcision was understood as an external sign of the interior covenant commitment (cf. Gen 17:9-14). To possess a circumcised heart was to have cast off sin and to have become submissive to God (cf. Lev 26:41; Dt 10:16; Jer 4:4). "The LORD your God will circumcise your heart and the heart of your offspring, so that you will love the LORD your God with all your heart and with all your soul, that you may live" (Dt 30:6). To be uncircumcised of heart, or uncircumcised of ear was to be rebellious (cf. Jer 6:10; 9:26; Ezek 44:7,9). Circumcision was then the outward sign of an interior freedom or separation from sin and thus of being set apart for God. Circumcision gave evidence that a person had become part of God's holy people (*Qahal yahweh*; in the Septuagint, *ekklesia*). However, while the Israelites were circumcised in the flesh, they were often uncircumcised in heart (cf. Jer 9:25-26). They were not fully cut free from sin or truly set apart for God. Within the Pauline tradition, this inherited Jewish understanding of circumcision formed the basis for and the prefigurement of what took place on the cross and what continues to transpire within baptism (see Rom 2:29).

Our "body of flesh" is put off in the "circumcision of Christ," that is, through his death on the cross. The cross is the true circumcision, "the new covenant in [his] blood" prefigured in the Old Testament, by which Christ was cut free of sin and all its effects, and was separated unto God (1 Cor 11:25).

Christians (Rom 8:9). Here in this world, the Christian already possesses the Spirit of God, which is a foretaste of the heavenly realm. We are transformed from sinners into children of God (Rom 8:15). We have a present share in the future eschatological reality. The Spirit will raise our mortal bodies to life as he did Christ's (Rom 8:11,22-23). See Kümmel, 212-20; also Fitzmyer, 1412-13.

Only if Jesus partook of our "flesh," a humanity weakened by sin and cursed by death, could he, on the cross, and in consequence we through baptism, be cut free of sin and its effects. Thus our "sacramental" circumcision (baptism) is again predicated upon the circumcision of Jesus' flesh, the death of a humanity contaminated with the effects of sin.[3] Likewise, in the resurrection of the new humanity of Christ, we through baptism are separated unto the holiness of God.

He Became Sin

Paul interpreted the significance of the Incarnation in light of these same soteriological premises. In Galatians, he wrote: "When the time had fully come, God sent forth his Son, born of woman, born under the law, to redeem those who were under the law, so that we might receive adoption as sons" (Gal 4:4-5). Paul accentuated that the Son was born of woman, thus sharing a common humanity with all who are born of women.[4] However, within the biblical tradition, "to be born of a woman" also carried with it negative implications. For example: "How then can man be righteous before God? How can he who is born of woman be clean?" (Jb 25:4; cf. 14:1; 15:14-16; Eccl 5:15-17). For Jesus to be born of a woman then meant that he too shared in our uncleanliness. He bore the trials and endless toil associated with sin and evil. This truth is strongly reinforced by what Paul said next: Jesus was born "under the law."

[3] Interestingly, Jesus spoke of his impending death as a baptism, a putting off of the old and putting on of the new (cf. Mk 10:30; Lk 12:50). We will speak more about this later.

[4] There is discussion as to whether Paul saw the Son to be pre-existent in this passage. While not explicit, the pre-existence could be implied. See Joseph Fitzmyer, *The New Jerome Biblical Commentary*, 787. See also F.F. Bruce, *Commentary on Galatians* (NIGTC) (Grand Rapids: Eerdmans, 1982), 195.

God promulgated the law as a constraint to and a guardian of our sinful drives. However, it became our curse for it incessantly exposed our sinfulness and moral impotency. Thus the law became our condemnation. For Paul, though Jesus was ever obedient to the law (which was his and is our righteousness), yet he, too, as a Jew and as a human person, was born under the law's curse, condemnation, guardianship, and enslavement (cf. Gal 3:13, 23-26).[5] Significantly, the Son did not become a man isolated from our sinful condition and, then, in an act of free moral solidarity, identify with our plight, taking on our sin and its effects; rather in the Incarnation, he personally became as we are—a son of the race of Adam, "descended from David according to the flesh" (Rom 1:3; cf. 2 Tim 2:8).

Paul confirmed this truth in Rom 8:3. There, he stated that God sent his "Son in the likeness of sinful flesh."[6] This is not a docetic statement, as if the Son only appeared to be in our likeness but really was not. However, in using the word "likeness" (*homoiomati*), did Paul wish to emphasize Jesus' similarity or dissimilarity to us? Did Paul mean to say that Jesus took on the appearance or guise of sinful flesh, but not the reality? Or did he mean that Jesus assumed the reality of sinful flesh and thus actually and visibly bore our likeness?

Paul consistently used "likeness" to denote appropriate correspondence or congruity (cf. Rom 1:23; 5:14; 6:5; Phil

---

[5] Cf. R. Schulte, *Mysterium Salutis,* Vol. 11 (Paris: Les Editions du Cerf, 1975), 377-78.

[6] In an excellent article, Vincent Branick argues that Paul's use of the word "sending" (*pempsas*), when preceded by God as the subject and the Son as the object, normally implies subjection or contamination (cf. Gal 4:4). See "The Sinful Flesh of the Son of God (Rom 8:3): A Key Image of Pauline Theology," *The Catholic Biblical Quarterly* 47 (1985), 247-48. I am indebted to Branick for helping clarify and expand some of my thinking concerning this verse and its implications.

2:7). Thus Paul affirmed Jesus' radical conformity to and solidarity with our sinful flesh (*sarx*). He too knew the dominion of sinful flesh made visible on the cross where that flesh was condemned (cf. Rom 8:3-4). Our sinful condition was made manifest and fully exposed in and through Jesus' humanity.[7]

Similarly, Paul stated, "For our sake he [God] made him to be sin who knew no sin" (2 Cor 5:21). Though Jesus never sinned (cf. Heb 4:15; 1 Pet 2:22; Jn 8:46; 1 Jn 3:5), yet God made him as sin in that the Son assumed both our sinful human condition in the Incarnation and, in his death, the full weight of our sin and condemnation.[8] On the cross, he stood

[7] This interpretation of Rom 8:3 differs slightly and yet significantly from the traditional understanding. The common interpretation would stress the dissimilarity between Jesus and ourselves without denying his true likeness to our sinful flesh. Thus Paul affirmed here that the eternal Son did assume our sinful condition and so could experience the effects of sin, but without himself becoming, like the rest of us, a sinner. Because Jesus did not personally sin, his sinful flesh is like but not identical to ours. See C.E.B. Cranfield, *The Epistle to the Romans*, Vol. I (Edinburgh: T. & T. Clark, 1975), 370-82; C.H. Dodd, *The Epistle of Paul to the Romans* (MNTC) (New York: Harper & Row, 1959), 119-20; J. Fitzmyer, *The New Jerome Biblical Commentary*, 822; S. Lyonnet, *Exegesis Epistulae Ad Romanos: Caput VIII* (Romae: Pontificium Institutum Biblicum, 1962), 6-7. While agreeing with this interpretation, I would want to emphasize with Branick that "the sense of the word (likeness) in Rom 8:3, therefore, by no means marks a distinction or a difference between Christ and sinful flesh. If Christ comes *en homoiomati* of sinful flesh, he comes as the full expression of that sinful flesh. He manifests it for what it is. Sinful flesh is fully visible in the flesh of Christ" (p. 250).

Interestingly. this verse is the antiphon used for the Canticle of Zechariah in the Morning Office for the Solemnity of the Annunciation, March 25. In prayer, the Church professes that the eternal Son was conceived in the likeness of our sinful flesh.

[8] Branick forcefully argues that "him" in "he [the Father] made him to be sin... " refers to the pre-existent Son. This verse would then be interpreted that although the eternal Son did not know sin as God, the Father, through the Incarnation, gave his Son a humanity contaminated by sin (cf. pp. 252-55).

before God as one like ourselves, as a sinner, and as such he offered his life as a sin offering to the Father.[9]

Second Cor 8:9 then should be interpreted in light of 5:21. As Jesus became sin for us that we might take on the righteousness of God, so he became poor for us not just economically, or even in the taking on of "a humanity," but in assuming the true poverty of our sinful condition. (Human beings without sin are not impoverished.) In so doing, he made us rich in eternal life. The impoverished Jesus, made poor in our sinful condition, is God's "inexpressible gift" to us (2 Cor 9:15).

We can then interpret the christological hymn in Phil 2:6-11 analogously. The one who was in the form of God emptied himself, not in the giving up of his divinity or in the arresting of some divine attributes (classical kenotic Christology), but in assuming the condition of a servant or slave. Thus he who was powerful in the likeness of God was now powerless in the "likeness of men" (*en homoiomati anthropon*). Within the context of the hymn, "the likeness of human beings" is "the condition of a slave," that is, humanity is in bondage to spiritual powers—sin, fear, and death (cf. Gal 4:1-11; 4:21-5:1; Rom 8:15).

Moreover, the term "slave" or "serant" recalls the Suffering Servant hymns of Deutero-Isaiah, especially 53:12: "He poured out his soul to death, and was numbered with the transgressors; yet he bore the sin of many, and made intercession for the transgressors." Jesus' death on the cross was an inherent

[9] Cf. J. Fitzmyer, *The New Jerome Biblical Commentary*, p. 822. Within the Catholic tradition, this passage is interpreted as Jesus' being a "sin offering" rather than as "sin". Nonetheless, Jesus could be a sin offering only if he became like one of us. As sin offerings (bulls and lambs) in the Old Testament figuratively stood in the place of the sinners, so Jesus became in reality what these offerings symbolized (cf. Lev 4:1-5:13). Cf. Branick, p. 256.

consequence (though freely and obediently embraced) of his appropriation of our sinful human condition.[10]

Putting Sin to Death

Thus far, we have shown that the Son assumed our "sinful flesh" and it was that flesh that died on the cross.[11] This is the foolish wisdom of God manifested in the human life of Jesus (cf. 1 Cor 1:20-31). But why did Jesus' death, the foolishness of God, have such radical consequences—"our righteousness and sanctification and redemption" (1 Cor 1:30)?

Firstly, the cross is not the passive killing of our "old self." Jesus did not simply endure the cross. The holy Son of God actively and willingly owned our condemnation and death—the curse of the law (cf. Gal 3:13). This he could not have authentically done in truth if he had not already shared our sinful condition.

Secondly, having assumed the curse of our condemnation, the Son freely, under the impulse of the Spirit, offered his holy and innocent human life—a life without personal sin, a life of perfect filial obedience—to the Father in expiation for sin.

This two-fold action of Jesus on the cross won for us forgiveness and life:

Then as one man's trespass led to condemnation for all men, so one man's act of righteousness leads to acquittal and life for all men. For as by one man's disobedience many were made sinners, so by one man's obedience many will be made righteous. (Rom 5:18-19).

[10] Cf. B. Byrne, *The New Jerome Biblical Commentary*, p.794.
[11] Branick concludes: "The earthly life of Jesus, telescoped into the crucifixion, is placed under the rubric of 'sin'" (p. 256).

Disobedience, a free human action, severed us from the Father and fashioned us into sinners. Inherently, disobedience is an act of rebellion and thus of separation. It is antithetical to love and so an affront to the all-holy and benevolent God. Therefore, sin is the supreme injustice, an act of absolute unrighteousness making us unrighteous and so ensuring our condemnation.

In contrast, the Son of God, as one impoverished by our sinful condition, through his free human obedience to the Father, even to death on the cross, made us righteous (cf. 2 Cor 5:21), nailing our condemnation to the cross (cf. Col 2:14). Jesus' obedient death on the cross was an act of supreme love to the Father, thus making just reparation for our spiteful and rebellious affront to the all-loving God. Through the blood of Jesus, we have peace with God (cf. Rom 3:25; 5:9; Col 1:20): "In him we have redemption through his blood, the forgiveness of our trespasses" (Eph 1:7). He did for us what we could not do for ourselves: "One has died for all; therefore all have died" (2 Cor 5:14).

Accordingly Jesus, in offering his human life on the cross as a holy and loving sacrifice to the Father, not only reconciled us to the Father, but, simultaneously, actively put to death our sinful flesh. This is important both for understanding the extent to which our humanity has been defiled by sin and for appreciating what Jesus did in assuming our fallen nature and putting it to death on the cross.

The cross depicts the full depravity of our sinful condition apart from Christ. While the Israelites in the Old Testament knew they were sinful and while the Gentiles (both yesterday and today) recognized that human nature is impaired and defaced, neither fathomed the full extent of humanity's desperate situation. The cross graphically illustrates that, while we were indeed redeemable, we could be salvaged only through the actual putting to death of the humanity inherited from

Adam. Sin had so thoroughly penetrated and contaminated our humanity that it had to die and be re-created. The cross, the putting to death of the flesh (*sarx*), is then the hermeneutical principle for understanding the radical sinfulness of our human condition. If Jesus had not crucified our sinful flesh, we would never have comprehended the full impact that sin had upon us, or have known the extent of God's love: "While we were still weak, at the right time Christ died for the ungodly. . . . God shows his love for us in that while we were yet sinners Christ died for us (Rom 5:6,8).[12]

We clearly perceive now how important it was for Paul that Jesus assumed our fallen condition and how significant were the loving and autonomous actions he performed within it. Moreover, it is equally significant that the Father raised Jesus from the dead.

Living in Christ: A New Kind Of Life

The risen Jesus is still a man, though now a glorious man freed from sin and all its effects.[13] That the Son continues to exist as a whole and entire man, though risen, is absolutely essential for understanding Paul's theology of baptism and for appreciating our salvation (cf. 2 Cor 13:4). Only in the resurrection did Jesus himself inherit the heavenly and imperishable (1 Cor 15:50). If Jesus had not been raised as a man, there would be no new humanity into which we could be baptized: "For as many of you as were baptized into Christ have put on Christ"

---

[12] The cross then is also the hermeneutical foundation for the doctrine of original sin. The cross proclaims that the inherited humanity in which we were born (as too was Jesus) is so contaminated by sin and so deprived of righteousness that it must die and be re-created in the risen Christ.

[13]. See 1 Cor 15:42ff. for Paul's distinction between the earthly and heavenly body. While Paul speaks of the heavenly body as being spiritual, it is nonetheless a true *body* of which he speaks.

(Gal 3:27). In baptism, we come to share in the risen life, in the new humanity of Jesus, and thus we too are "alive to God in Christ Jesus" (Rom 6:11). As Jesus assumed the condition of our fallen ancestor Adam and put it to death, so now, as risen, he is the new Adam, the author of a new humanity (cf. 1 Cor 15:22,45). Thus we no longer need live by the flesh, but we can live by the Spirit, that is, by the new life we now live in Christ (cf. Rom 8).

Having come to live in the risen Christ through sharing in his death, Paul and the early Christian communities experienced a three-fold effect. They believed that Jesus had radically altered our relationship with God and with one another, and that concurrently we were re-created. This very experience, as we stated earlier, helped them to perceive the marvelous transformation that Jesus accomplished in his death and resurrection.

Firstly, through Jesus' death and resurrection, our relationship with God did not just improve by degree, but substantially changed in kind: "There is no condemnation for those who are in Christ Jesus" (Rom 8:1). No longer need our sin fashion us into enemies of God. Rather through faith and baptism, we are justified, and made righteous and holy before God (cf. Rom 1:17; 3:28; 4:5; Gal 2:16; 3:8; Phil 3:9). We are transformed by the indwelling Spirit of the Son into children of the Father. Calling out "*Abba*, Father," we can share in the same intimacy with the Father as Jesus the Son (cf. Gal 4:6; Rom 8:15). The Spirit reveals within us the filial love the Father has for us (cf. Rom 5:5). This is the new and singular privilege of the Christian.

Secondly, our relationship with fellow Christians is substantially different from the relationship we have with those who are not. Christians living in Christ become members of his body and thus their relationship with one another changes not in degree but in kind. Together with Christ, we truly share a common and distinctive life and unity formed by the Spirit. We are brothers and sisters in Christ (cf. Rom 12:4-5; 1 Cor 12:12-13; Eph 2:11-22). So dramatically has our relationship changed that there is "neither Jew nor Greek, there is neither slave nor free, there is neither male nor female; for you are all one in Christ Jesus" (Gal 3:28; cf. Rom 10:12; 1 Cor 12:13; Col 3:11). Even such elemental relationships as husband and wife, parents and children, and master and slave have been placed on an entirely new level (cf. Eph 5:21-6:9; Col 3:18-4:1; Phlm).

Lastly, we ourselves have changed, not in degree, but in kind. Paul declared: "I have been crucified with Christ; it is no longer I who live, but Christ who lives in me" (Gal 2:20; see 6:14). He even said that he bore the brandmarks of Christ, the signs of his dying and rising with him (cf. Gal 6:17; 2 Cor 4:10). A Christian is a different kind of person. While Christians remain human persons of the same physical nature as those who have not converted, yet there is a substantial change within them and not just one of degree.

This substantial change within us who believe is due to our now living in Christ, sharing in his resurrected humanity in all its glory: "Therefore, if anyone is in Christ, he is a new creation; the old has passed away, behold, the new has come" (2 Cor 5:17). We "put off [the] old nature" and "put on the new nature, created after the likeness of God in true righteousness and holiness" (Eph 4:22-24).

The indwelling of the Spirit transforms us: "You are not in the flesh, you are in the Spirit, if in fact the Spirit of God dwells in you (Rom 8:9; cf. 8:11). Where we were once sinners (in the flesh), now we are holy and righteous. We are temples, the very holy of holies (*naos*), where the Holy Spirit resides (cf. 1 Cor 3:16-17; 6:19).[14]

---

[14] Many contemporary theologies of salvation understand Jesus as bringing about changes only in degree. Our relationship with God changes

We have purposely stressed the singular and substantial effects of dying and rising with Christ. Too frequently today, people assume that every person of good will or of any religious persuasion has a similar or identical relationship with God. While we cannot judge the subjective, spiritual condition of any individual, Christians do believe that those who are in Christ have a relationship with the Father that radically differs from those who do not live in Christ. To dismiss this fundamental newness would be to subvert and diminish what the Son of God freely accomplished as man, through his obedient death on the cross and in his resurrection.

Moreover, today, we often do not appreciate how our relationships within the body of Christ, within the Church, are unique. We assume that Christian relationships are merely based on human friendship or upon an intensified feeling of *esprit de corps* common among the global family. Again, this depreciation of the distinctive nature of Christian relationships is founded upon a cheapening of what the historical Jesus did through his death, and what it means now to share in his risen humanity.

Likewise, people undervalue the substantial change that takes place within a person upon Christian conversion. The commonly held assumption is that human beings are basically good and thus Jesus only helps us become better. We also depreciate the historical Jesus and what he did as man. Within this view, Jesus, through his human actions, does not make possible our radical re-creation in the Spirit. But Christians,

in degree but not in kind. Process theology is a good example of this type of soteriology. Cf. Norman Pittenger, *Process Thought and Christian Faith* (New York: Macmillan, 1968) and *Christology Reconsidered* (London: SCM, 1970); also David Griffin, *A Process Christology* (Philadelphia: Westminster Press, 1973). For a critique, see Weinandy, *Does God Change?*, pp. 151-52; also Donald Bloesch, "Process Theology in a Reformed Perspective," *Listening* 14 (1979) 191.

within the regenerate faculty of their own spirit, live by the holy and transforming power of the Spirit—a power that is beyond the simply human (cf. Rom 8).

We must take seriously the revolutionary nature of taking on the new humanity of Jesus and, with it, the new mind formed by the indwelling Spirit (cf. 1 Cor 2). We are to appropriate godly attitudes and motivations, and in faith live by the truths of the Gospel. Such revelation comes personally to Christians in and through the Spirit and is remote or even inaccessible to those outside of Christ. Thus Christians do not set their minds on the things of the flesh, but "set their minds on the things of the Spirit" (Rom 8:5). The Spirit of Christ revives our spirit (cf. Rom 8:9). Unlike unbelievers, our minds need not be "conformed to this world" with its self-centered and egotistical agenda, with its darkness and spurning of the truth. Rather we can be "transformed by the renewal of [our] minds", so that we prove "what is the will of God, what is good and acceptable and perfect" (Rom 12:2).

This is the heart of the Christian life—the call to holiness. Founded upon the crucifixion of our sinful nature in Jesus and his rising to newness of life, we daily put sin, the *sarx*, to death and live by the Spirit, our new life in Christ: "If by the Spirit you put to death the deeds of the body you will live" (Rom 8:13). Thus, a Christian is not just a noble moral person, but an entirely new creation in the Holy Spirit having put to death the old self in Christ and, now, in Christ, being alive to God (cf. 2 Cor 5:17). We are God's workmanship, created in Christ "for good works" (Eph 2:10).

Moreover, because Jesus put to death our sinful nature and acquired a risen humanity, Christians, unlike unbelievers, live in anticipation of his return in glory and the fulfillment of our transformation now begun in him (cf. 1 Cor 15). As our present life transcends merely human life, so our goal exceeds that of the simply human and finite. We have been "sealed with the promised Holy Spirit, which is the guarantee of our inheritance until we acquire possession of it, to the praise of his glory" (Eph 1:14; cf. 2 Cor 1:22). Living in Christ, we find that our whole perspective on life is changed. Our mind must be set on heaven and the things of God (cf. 2 Cor 4:18):

> If then you have been raised with Christ, seek the things that are above, where Christ is, seated at the right hand of God. Set your minds on things that are above, not on things that are on earth. For you have died, and your life is hid with Christ in God. When Christ who is our life appears, then you also will appear with him in glory. (Col 3:1-4).

Our goal is established upon the truth of our thesis—our old life, our sinful humanity, has died with Christ, and now in him, we live in the hope of future glory: "If the Spirit of him who raised Jesus from the dead dwells in you, he who raised Christ Jesus from the dead will give life to your mortal bodies also through his Spirit which dwells in you" (Rom 8:11). What was sown in perishability, dishonor, and weakness (that is, in sin and death—our and Jesus' humanity) will be raised as imperishable, in glory, and the fullness of power (cf. 1 Cor 15:42-44,53-54): "Just as we [including Jesus] have borne the image of the man of dust, we shall also bear the image of the man of heaven" (1 Cor 15:49).

Our study of the Pauline corpus then has taught us: (1) the Son of God assumed our fallen humanity, freely putting it to death on the cross in loving atonement to the Father. (Everything else is founded upon this.); (2) the Father raised him as a glorious man to be Lord; (3) through faith and baptism, we can share in this transformation of Jesus' humanity. As human persons, we, too, can die and rise with Christ; (4) living now in Christ, we are made holy and righteous having new and distinctly Christian relationships with the Father and with our brothers and sisters in Christ; and (5) we anticipate his return in glory when we will come to the fullness of redemption so that "God may be everything to everyone" (1 Cor 15:28).

Addendum: The Humanity of Jesus in the First Letter of Peter

The First Letter of Peter contains some relevant passages for our study. Before we proceed, we will briefly examine them.

While 1 Peter states explicitly that Jesus was without sin, yet it likewise proclaims that he "himself bore our sins in his body [*hos tas hamartias emon autos anenegken en to somati autou*] on the tree, that we might die to sin and live to righteousness. By his wounds you have been healed" (1 Pet 2:23-24; cf. 2:22). This passage is reminiscent of Paul (cf. Rom 6:11,18; 2 Cor 5:21). As the Suffering Servant who bore our sin, he became sin in his own flesh in order that sin might be put to death on the cross (cf. Is 53:5-6,12). Thus, we are able to live as righteous men and women before God.

Peter then reconfirms the differentiation between Jesus, living in the flesh, that is, in our sinful earthly condition, and being raised to a new life free from sin and death.

Through baptism, we participate in this same transformation (cf. 1 Pet 1:3; 3:21-22). Christ died "for sins once for all" since he was "put to death in the flesh [*thanatotheis men sarki*] but made alive in the spirit" (1 Pet 3:18). Because Christ "suffered in the flesh [*pathontos sarki*]," he separated himself from sin. Thus, we too need no longer live by human passions, but "by the will of God" (1 Pet 4:1-3).[15]

---

[15] We should note that First Peter is also the source of the tradition that Jesus, after he died, went to preach to the "spirits in prison, who formerly did not obey" (1 Pet 3:19).

CHAPTER SEVEN

THE HUMAN MYSTERIES OF THE SON

Keeping in mind what we have learned from our study of Paul, we want now to examine other New Testament testimony concerning the mysteries of Jesus' human life—specifically his baptism, temptations, miracles, transfiguration, and agony in the garden.

These events or mysteries, while distinct, compose and shape the whole of Jesus' life, and so express and embody the undivided mystery which is Christ himself—the mystery of God (cf. Eph 1:3-10).[1] Thus, we can comprehend them only within the context of Jesus' entire life, especially his death and

---

[1] We will continue to follow, as far as possible, the order of faith and knowledge and not the order of chronology. For this reason, we will examine the infancy narratives and those passages which speak specifically of the Incarnation (for example, Jn 1 and Heb 1) after we study the rest of Jesus' life. Contemporary Scripture scholars argue that these passages, while first in the order of chronology, were some of the last to be formulated and written (see Raymond E. Brown, *The Birth of the Messiah* [Garden City, NY: Doubleday, 1977], 25-41). Only in light of Jesus' earthly life, and especially as a consequence of his death and resurrection, did the early Church grasp the full significance of what had already taken place at Jesus' conception and birth. We should not think that the early Church "fabricated" the events of his conception and birth in light of the cross and resurrection, but rather used these later events of Jesus' earthly life as the interpretive tool for understanding the true nature of what had happened at the beginning of his life (see René Laurentin, *The Truth of Christmas* [Petersham, MA: St. Bede's Publications, 1986]).

resurrection. In turn, the early Christian tradition and the evangelists recognized that the whole mystery of Christ, especially his death and resurrection, can be fully appreciated only in light of them. The Gospel writers employ these events to advance, by way of prophetic prefigurement and anticipation, the paschal mystery itself.[2] Here, we wish to discern how these events in the earthly life of Jesus help us appreciate his fallen humanity and what he accomplished as man.

The Baptism of Jesus

All three Synoptic Gospels treat John's baptism of Jesus. The Acts of the Apostles mentions it, while the Gospel of John and the Letter to the Hebrews allude to it (Mk 1:9-11; Mt 3:11-17; Lk 3:21-22; Acts 1:22, 10:37; Jn 1:32-34; Heb 3:2). These multiple references show that the early Church saw the baptism of Jesus as highly significant. It recognized that in and through his baptism, Jesus was thrust into his public ministry which would culminate in his death and resurrection. Thus, the first Christians discerned, as we will see, that Jesus' baptism prophetically anticipated his entire work of salvation.

To Fulfill All Righteousness

The Gospel of Mark states that John came "preaching a baptism of repentance for the forgiveness of sin" (Mk 1:4). People from all the Judean countryside and "all the people of Jerusalem" came to him: "They were baptized in [en] the river Jordan" (Mk 1:5). Likewise, "in those days Jesus came from

---

[2] See A. Grillmeier, "Les Mystères de la Vie de Jesus," *Mysterium Salutis*, Vol. 11 (Paris: Les Editions Du Cerf, 1975), 329-57; R. Schulte, "Les Mystères de la 'Prehistoire' de Jesus," *Ibid.*, 359-402; K. Rahner, *Theological Investigations*, Vol. 7 (New York: Herder and Herder, 1971). Rahner devotes essays to specific mysteries (pp. 121-201); Hans Urs von Balthasar, *Mysterium Paschale*, 41.

Nazareth of Galilee and was baptized by John in [*eis*] the river Jordan" (Mk 1:9). For Mark, Jesus was not just baptized physically in (*en*) the river Jordan, but his baptism was a baptism into (*eis*)—an immersing, a becoming one with—all that the river Jordan now signified—an identification with our sinfulness and the need for repentance.[3] He was one with the whole of Judea and all the people of Jerusalem. The Gospel of Luke also emphasizes Jesus' affinity with us: "Now when *all* the people were baptized, and when Jesus *also* had been baptized. . . " (Lk 3:21) (emphasis added).

The Gospel of Matthew, in light of this identification, raises what must have been an important and even embarrassing question for the early Christians. If Jesus was holy and sinless, why did he receive John's baptism, a baptism of repentance?

Then Jesus came from Galilee to the Jordan to John, to be baptized by him. John would have prevented him, saying, "I need to be baptized by you, and do you come to me?" But Jesus answered him, "Let it be so now; for thus it is fitting for us to fulfill all righteousness." Then he consented. (Mt 3:13-15).

John the Baptist was right: he did need Jesus to baptize him, but that could not be done until after Jesus died and rose, i.e., after all righteousness was fulfilled. Only then would what had begun there be completed so that the Spirit could be poured out (cf. Jn 7:39).

Here Jesus accepted John's baptism, thus identifying with us. However, we must not construe Jesus' identification with our sinful condition as purely voluntary, as if he had no inherent need for John's baptism, but proceeded only to affirm

[3] See C. Schutz, "Les Mystères de la Vie Publique De Jesus," *Mysterium Salutis*, Vol. 11, 414-22.

freely his solidarity with our situation. Rather, while Jesus had not sinned, yet he had assumed our sinful nature; and thus as a man he, too, as truly one of us, was obliged to respond to John's call to repentance and baptism. (Take note that Jesus took himself *to* John along with all the other sinners; cf. Mt 3:13.)

In the future, Jesus would have no need of John's baptism. He would be the baptizer in the Holy Spirit and thus surpass John's baptism of repentance. But "now. . .it is fitting for us to fulfill all righteousness," that is, now Jesus must stand firm against temptation and sin. The Son of God, as man, must live as a righteous, obedient Son of the Father and thus fulfill the law (cf. Mt 5:17). He must die and rise. His humanity must be transformed. Jesus recognized that this is ultimately the baptism, the righteousness which the baptism in the Jordan prefigured, which he must undergo and anxiously awaits (Mk 10:38-39; Lk 12:50).

The Spirit of Obedience

The full significance of Jesus' baptism is manifested only if it anticipates the cross not just figuratively but intrinsically. But this inborn affinity is secured only if Jesus' humanity is one with ours—a humanity in need of transformation and rebirth.

> Matthew continues:
> And when Jesus was baptized, he went up immediately from the water, and behold, the heavens were opened and he saw the Spirit of God descending like a dove, and alighting on him; and lo, a voice from heaven, saying, "This is my beloved Son, with whom I am well pleased". (Mt 3:16-17).

To argue that prior to his baptism, Jesus did not possess the Spirit would be erroneous. However, it would be equally mistaken to maintain that the Spirit did not come upon him in a new and real way at his baptism. The baptism was more than divine theatrics.

The dominant Jewish belief at the time was that God had been silent since the last prophet. The heavens had been closed. Now with the baptism of Jesus, the Father had torn open (*schizomenous* in Mk 1:10) the heavens and sent forth his Spirit. Through this anointing of the Spirit, the Father commissioned the earthly Jesus to inaugurate the kingdom of God. Once more, there would be access to the Father.[4]

The Spirit, portrayed as a dove coming upon Jesus, recalls the imagery of the first creation story (Gn 1:1-2).[5] There, the Spirit hovered over the watery abyss. Here, he hovers over the river Jordan and new life again comes forth. Jesus the possessor of the Holy Spirit, who is now one with the old creation, will be the author of the new creation. He will become the new Adam through the death of his old humanity and the birth of his new risen nature.

The words the Father speaks are from Ps 2:7 ("You are my beloved son") and from Is 42:1 ("Behold my servant, in whom

---

[4] This tearing open of the heavens finds its ultimate symbol in the rending of the curtain in the temple, the splitting open of the rocks, and the opening of the tombs of the saints at the moment of Jesus' death (cf. Mt 27:51-53). Because of Jesus' death (his true baptism), the saints and all who believe have access once more to the heavenly realm—to the very presence of God. The Letter to the Hebrews speaks of the reality of this rending which Jesus' baptism prefigured and the torn temple curtain symbolized: "the new and living way which he opened for us through the curtain, that is through his flesh" (Heb 10:20). We will examine further the curtain of Jesus' flesh in the next chapter.

[5] See C. Schutz, *Mysterium Salutis*, 11, 410. He notes that in both the creation story of Gn 1:1 and the baptism of Jesus, there is "l'Eau, l'Esprit et la Voix." We see similar imagery also in the dove that Noah sent out from the ark (Gn 8:10-12).

I am well pleased").[6] Psalm 2 is a kingly enthronement psalm and thus the Father declared that Jesus was his Son whom he would enthrone over the whole earth (v. 8). However, Jesus will be enthroned only because he would be the loyal, obedient servant of the Father. The Isaiah passage is the opening verse of the first of four Suffering Servant songs from Deutero-Isaiah: "Behold my servant, whom I uphold, my chosen, in whom my soul delights; I have put my Spirit upon him, he will bring forth justice to the nations" (Is 42:1). There is also an allusion to Gn 22:2. God told Abraham:

> Take your son, your only son Isaac, whom you love, and go to the land of Moriah, and offer him there as a burnt offering upon one of the mountains of which I shall tell you.

What God ultimately did not allow Abraham to do, that is, sacrifice his only, beloved son, God himself will do. In Jesus' baptism, the Father is preparing the sacrifice of his beloved Son.[7]

We see here the fusion of the concepts of Son (Ps 2:7; Gn 22:2) and Servant (Is 42:1). Within the Synoptic tradition,

---

[6] The three Synoptic Gospels differ as to what the Father says. In Mark, the baptism of Jesus is narrated as something almost exclusively for himself—Jesus alone sees the heavens open and the Father's words are addressed to him in the second person—"You are my beloved Son" (Mk 1:9-11; cf. Lk 3:21-22). In Matthew, Jesus also sees the heavens open, but the Father's words are now addressed to the people: "This is my beloved Son...." (Mt 3:13-17). The oldest tradition would seem to be Mark (who influenced Luke) since it is unlikely that the early Church would address to Jesus something which the Father spoke to Jesus' disciples. However, we could surmise that the early Church recognized that what the Father had said to Jesus was something that they too needed to lay hold of in faith. See Benedict Viviano, O.P., *The New Jerome Biblical Commentary*, 637-38.

[7] See I. Howard Marshall, *Jesus the Savior: Studies in the New Testament* (Downers Grove, IL: InterVarsity Press, 1990), 120-33.

Jesus' divine Sonship will be revealed only through his being a servant.

Jesus was then anointed with the Spirit so that he might be, under our fallen condition, an obedient servant and thus bring forth justice and righteousness. Through his obedient suffering, he would learn and testify to what it means to be the Son of the Father (cf. Is 52:13-53:12 and Heb 5:8). The Father, then, at Jesus' baptism, confirmed his vocation which he had prepared for him when he sent him into the world and created for him a humanity like our own.

Moreover, the fact that the Son assumed our fallen condition lends greater importance to the truth that Jesus actually needed the Spirit. The Spirit by which he is eternally the faithful, divine Son of the Father is the same Spirit which molded and sealed his humanity, and empowered him, as man, to live as the loyal Son.

Within John's Gospel, the Baptist stressed that the one upon whom the Spirit descended would baptize in the Holy Spirit, that he would be the Son of God (Jn 1:31-34). At first, there seems to be no hint of Jesus' solidarity with ourselves. However, Jesus manifested his true Sonship and became the baptizer in the Spirit only because he took upon himself our sin and obediently offered himself as a cleansing sacrifice on our behalf. John the Baptist proclaimed that the Son of God who would so baptize is the Lamb of God who takes away the sins of the world (cf. Jn 1:29). Jesus as the Lamb of God reminds us of the Suffering Servant upon whom will be laid our iniquity (cf. Is 53:7; Acts 8:32) and the passover lamb whose blood will cleanse us of sin and death (cf. Ex 12:46; Jn 19:36).[8] Typically, John has given here a theological interpretation to the Synoptic account of Jesus' baptism.

---

[8] See R. Brown, *The Gospel According to John,* Vol. 1, 58-67.

Jesus' baptism then highlights both his identity with our sinful humanity and how, through his obedient life, he would bring forth our salvation. Thus, Jesus' baptism anticipates all the future challenges and temptations within his life, prefiguring the ultimate test of his passion and death. Moreover, we see here, more clearly than in Paul, the important role the Holy Spirit played within Jesus' humanity.

The Temptations of Jesus

The Letter to the Hebrews assures us that we, in our weakness and sin, can approach "the throne of grace" with confidence because Jesus is merciful and understanding: "For we have not a high priest who is unable to sympathize with our weaknesses, but one who in every respect has been tempted as we are, yet without sin" (Heb 4:15-16; cf. 2:18).

Jesus' temptations verify that he genuinely assumed our human condition. Otherwise, he could not sympathize with our weakness, which is due to sin. Even though he possessed singular grace and power, he nonetheless was not immune from the attacks of Satan. The temptations of Jesus, those in the desert at the onset of his ministry (which we will examine shortly) as well as his daily temptations culminating in the garden of Gethsemane, do pose, however, a unique problem.

Temptation presupposes enticement. There must be a lure and an attraction. For example, temptations of lust and greed allure us by the good and pleasure they offer. Our concupiscence conspires with external stimuli to give rise to temptation. We observe an attractive woman or man, or notice an expensive car. Our already corrupted passions connive with these allurements to tempt us with lust or greed. Our memory and imagination in turn spawn temptations. Jesus appears to be in a different situation.

While Jesus assumed our fallen condition and thus could be tempted, yet (according to later theological tradition and development) he was filled with the Spirit from conception, thereby freeing him from the morally corrupting effects of original sin. Even though the New Testament does not make any distinction between temptations that arise from "outside" and those that originate from "within" a person (cf. Jas 1:1-3), the received tradition seems to demand that Jesus' temptations could not have risen from within him since he did not share our concupiscence, i.e., our propensity to sin.[9] Does this suggest that his temptations were less severe than our own, even to the point of being fictitious?

Exactly the reverse is true. Both because Jesus had taken on our fallen condition and thus was vulnerable to the attacks of Satan and because he was filled with the Spirit and thus had a clarity and holiness far exceeding our own, temptation confronted him with a sharpness and force we do not experience. Our minds and hearts are anesthetized and dulled by our concupiscence and personal sin. Moreover, because we almost inevitably conspire with the temptation to some degree, teasing it on, we never feel its full impact.[10] Jesus, however, with complete clarity and perception, experienced both the entire allurement of temptation and, because he never conspired with it, endured the undivided assault of Satan's attack. Thus, instead of envisioning the tempting of Jesus to be mere play acting, we should recognize that Satan tempted and attacked him with a ferocity that we never experience. We should also note that he conquered

---

[9] We noted earlier that St. Thomas Aquinas held that Jesus did not assume the "fomes" of sin, that is, our concupiscence. See *Summa Theologica,* III,15,2. Likewise, various councils of the Church have upheld Jesus' sinlessness and freedom from concupiscence. See ch. 4, note 31.

[10] The quickest and easiest way to alleviate the painful struggle of temptation is to give into it.

temptation as one of us, as a man who freely lived by the indwelling Spirit.[11]

Faithful as a Son

All of Jesus' temptations, as do all of ours, touched upon his faithfulness to God. Would he, as man, be the loyal Son? Would he be true to his messianic vocation? This is clearly seen in his temptations in the desert.

According to the Synoptic tradition, immediately following Jesus' commission to found God's kingdom, the Spirit led Jesus into the desert. Mark emphasizes that the Spirit drove (*ekballei*, to thrust forth forcibly) him out, implying that the Spirit was compelling Jesus to do battle with Satan and that only through the Spirit's power would he triumph and establish God's kingdom (Mk 1:12).[12]

Matthew and Luke, unlike Mark, specify the nature of Jesus' temptations. Here, we will concentrate primarily on Matthew's Gospel since it better serves our needs.

Matthew, writing for a Jewish audience, wished to portray Jesus as the New Israel and as the transformation from a sinful people to a holy people. As the New Israel, Jesus, the Son (presently in the flesh), was called from the sinful exile in Egypt (cf. Mt 2:15; Hos 11:1; Ex 4:22). His baptism in the river Jordan was reminiscent of Israel's crossing the Red Sea on its way to the promised land, the prefigurement of God's kingdom now to be inaugurated by Jesus. Lastly, as the Jews were tempted in the desert, so too was Jesus. However, unlike the

---

[11] According to our principle, the holier one becomes, the more intense will be one's temptations. The lives of the saints seem to bear this out.

[12] We see clearly in Mk 3:20-30 that Jesus triumphed over Satan through the power of the Spirit, whereas Jesus was accused of casting out Satan by the power of Satan. Jesus responded that such an accusation was a blasphemy against the Holy Spirit, the unforgivable sin.

Old Israel, Jesus, the New Israel, triumphed over the desert testing.[13]

After Jesus had fasted and prayed for forty days (symbolic of Israel's forty years), "the tempter came and said to him, 'If you are the Son of God, command these stones to become loaves of bread'" (Mt 4:1-3). Israel, God's son, murmured and grumbled in the desert for lack of bread, so now Jesus is also tempted by hunger. Unlike his ancestors, Jesus would be the true Son. (Notice that Satan's words, "If you are the Son of God," echo the Father's words at the baptism, "This is my beloved Son." Although Satan desired Jesus to prove his Sonship by vulgar displays of power, Jesus would manifest it by unassuming obedience.) He would live not by earthly bread, but would feed on God's word: "It is written 'Man shall not live by bread alone, but by every word that proceeds from the mouth of God'" (Mt 4:4; cf. Dt 8:3; Lk 4:3-4).[14]

Satan here proposed to Jesus, as the Son, a life of self-centered, earthly comfort and riches. He would likewise tempt him with self-aggrandizement, earthly power, and kingship (cf. Mt 4:7-10; Lk 4:5-8), thereby striking at the very heart of the Father's proclamation that, unlike the Israelites and all humankind, he was to be the humble, obedient Son who would be the Servant/Messiah.

Jesus withstood Satan's three temptations. His final remark is significant: "Begone, Satan! for it is written, 'You shall worship the Lord your God and him only shall you serve'" (Mt 4:10). Jesus' temptations looked to the future, to the ultimate

---

[13] Jesus responded to Satan by quoting from the book of Deuteronomy, thus joining himself to and contrasting himself with the Israelites in the desert (Dt 8:3; 6:13-16).

[14] We might also see here a contrast between Jesus and Adam and Eve. As the primordial sinners, they dd not live by God's word, but preferred the fruit of the tree of the knowledge of good and evil (Gn 2:15-17; 3:1-7).

temptation, that of rejecting or accepting the cup given him by the Father. Would Jesus honor and serve himself or be obedient to his Father?[15]

The Power of the Spirit

In perceiving the lies of Satan and withstanding his assaults, Jesus demonstrated that by the power of the Spirit, Satan had no control over him. On the contrary, he now had authority over Satan. Unlike the first Adam who did not adhere to the Spirit of truth but fell to the lies of Satan and was thus driven from paradise into the desert (cf. Gn 3:22-24), Jesus was here anticipating and emerging as the New Adam who is faithful to God, does not fall, and thus returns from the desert into the new paradise of God's kingdom.[16] This is why Hebrews notes that "he is able to help those who are tempted" (Heb 2:18). By fending off temptation, Jesus was reversing, in his own human mind, will, and emotions, the condition in which we, in our human psyche, have been bound by Satan since the Fall.

Jesus' temptations illustrate three important elements of our study. Firstly, Jesus assumed our human condition and as man was tempted. Secondly, as one of us, he warded off the assaults of Satan in and through the power of the Holy Spirit. Thirdly, he triumphed through genuine human obedience to the will of the Father, thus manifesting his authenticity as the Son. Each of these points finds its completion in the pascal mystery.

[15] Luke inverts Matthew's second and third temptation, thus having the last temptation take place in Jerusalem. Luke may have done this to suggest that the future (the more "opportune time") and ultimate temptation would take place in Jerusalem at the time of his passion and death (Lk 4:9-13).

[16] See C. Schutz, *Mysterium Salutis*, 11, 445-47. We could also conclude our previous analogy by stating that unlike the Old Israel, Jesus (the New Israel) has not fallen to Satan's desert temptations and so truly enters into the promised land—the new kingdom of God.

The Miracles

At first, Jesus' miracles do not appear to bear upon our thesis. Because they are exercises of power (*dynameis*) by which Jesus frees and delivers men and women from the evil due to sin—sickness, demon possession, death—the miracles do not seem to manifest the taking on of our weak, sinful condition. Instead, they seem to indicate precisely the opposite—through authority and might, Jesus casts off sin and its effects. However, the Gospel of Matthew grasps a profound insight into Jesus' miracles which relates directly to our subject.

Jesus as the Suffering Servant prophesied in Deutero-Isaiah is a key motif within Matthew's Gospel.[17] Matthew interpreted Jesus' miracles in this light:

That evening they brought to him many who were possessed with demons; and he cast out the spirits with a word, and healed all who were sick. This was to fulfill what was spoken by the prophet Isaiah, "He took our infirmities and bore our diseases". (Mt 8:16-17).

The comparison here looks forced and contrived for the reasons we already stated. However, on the cross, Jesus would adopt our infirmities and diseases due to sin, and thus free us from evil and restore us to health. The cross then is the ultimate display of power—*dynameis*—and the definitive source of healing and restoration. Therefore, Matthew perceived that Jesus, in and through his miracles, prophetically prefigured what was to take place on the cross—the taking on of our sin and the securing of our deliverance and healing. Moreover, only because of what transpired on the cross could Jesus, in his public ministry, heal men and women of sickness and free them from the power of Satan.

[17] See Benedict T. Viviano, *The New Jerome Biblical Commentary*, 684.

With this understanding of Jesus' miracles, we can discern
the significance of what we might at first not notice in some
miracle accounts. For example, the Synoptic accounts of the
healing of the leper (Mt 8:1-4; Mk 1:40-45; Lk 5:12-16) note
that Jesus "stretched out his hand and touched him [the
leper]". Such a "touching" contaminated Jesus with the disease
and made him ritually and socially impure.[18] However, Jesus
in this "touching" both identified himself with the man's
condition, and also vividly portrayed the truth that he was
taking upon himself the man's disease and social banishment.
In so doing, Jesus healed the man. On a deeper level, Jesus is
manifesting his identity with our sinful condition. We are
healed only because of this affiliation.

Paradoxically for Matthew and the other Synoptics, Jesus
through his miracles allied himself with our sinful condition,
for only through such a solidarity ultimately displayed on the
cross could he heal and restore us to life. Thus, the miracles
anticipate the work of the cross and are proleptically accomplished through its power.

The Transfiguration

The transfiguration of Jesus (cf. Mt 17:1-9; Mk 9:2-10; Lk
9:28-36; 2 Pet 1:17-18) integrates all that has gone before and
directs it to the future. In all three Synoptic accounts, Jesus is
transfigured immediately after Peter's profession of faith and
Jesus' first prediction of his passion. Peter contradicts Jesus
only to be told that he, like Satan, is tempting him with a view
of his vocation not in keeping with his Father's will.

Moreover, while all three Synoptics place the transfiguration within the context of Jesus' journey to Jerusalem, Luke
assigns special significance to this. He situates the transfiguration just prior to Jesus' setting "his face to go to Jerusalem" (Lk

[18] See R.J. Karris, O.F.M., *The New Jerome Biblical Commentary*, 692.

9:51; cf. 13:33, 19:11). The transfiguration for Luke then specifies the nature of Jesus' journey and anticipates what would take place in Jerusalem. Jesus set upon an exodus. He spoke with Moses and Elijah about "his departure [*exodon*]" (Lk 9:31). Through his death and resurrection, he would depart from this world into glory. Thus, the transfiguration cannot be understood apart from the pascal event for it prefigured and helped interpret it.

The setting of the transfiguration itself is reminiscent of Old Testament theophanies, especially those involving Moses. The glory of God, the *shekinah*, was manifested in the cloud and, like Moses, the flesh of Jesus was transformed into brilliant light, a reflection of the glory of God (cf. Ex 34:29,35). The Father's words likewise recall Jesus' baptism where he first commissioned and proclaimed him to be the Suffering Servant/Son (cf. Ps 2:7; Is 42:1; Dt 18:15). The Father again confirmed that Jesus is his loyal and faithful Son; the one he has chosen and anointed. His command though points us to the future. We are to listen to his Son (cf. Lk 9:35).[19] The Gospels imply that what the Father may have had specifically in mind was Jesus' previous prediction of his passion and death as well as the two predictions yet to come (cf. Lk 9:43-45; 18:31-32; Mt 17:22-23; 20:17-9; Mk 9:30-32; 10:32-34).

The Father's words thus imply that the ultimate transformation of Jesus would come through his filial obedience, specifically, his free acceptance of the cross. Jesus would obediently fulfill the old Law (symbolized by Moses) and the prophets (symbolized by Elijah) and, in so doing, fulfill the righteous will of his Father. Thus his present humanity, inherited from Adam, would be transfigured into a new humanity.

---

[19] 2 Pet 1:17 actually gives the Father's words at baptism and not the words of the transfiguration: "This is my beloved Son, with whom I am well pleased." Compare with Lk 9:35.

The transfiguration of Jesus is not primarily the revelation of his divinity, but a prophetic dramatization of his cross and resurrection, his human exodus from sin and death to freedom and life. It is founded then upon the premise that Jesus assumed our fallen condition and was transforming it through Spirit- empowered human action—obedience—into a new humanity.[20]

Gethsemane

Jesus' experience in the garden of Gethsemane brought to completion, and thus fully illustrates, what had begun at and was prefigured in his baptism and temptations in the desert—Jesus' full human condition and his filial obedience nurtured by the Spirit.

At his baptism, Jesus was commissioned by the Father to be the Servant/Son. In the desert, Satan tested his loyalty to this commission. Now in the garden, Jesus encountered the ultimate and consummate trial (cf. Mt 26:36-46; Mk 14:32-42; Lk 22:39-46; Jn 12:27). He confronted the prospect of his imminent passion and death. As a man, living under the conditions of sin, such a prospect seemed overwhelming. His soul was "very sorrowful, even to death" (Mt 26:38; cf. Mk 14:34; Ps 42:6). While his humanity shrunk from the cross, yet the Spirit of Sonship strengthened his resolve. The Son of God in the frailty of his humanity prayed, "Abba, Father, all things are possible to you; remove this cup from me; yet not what I will, but what you will" (Mk 14:36).

---

[20] For Paul, the glory of the risen Jesus, prefigured here in the transfiguration and reminiscent of Moses' splendor, can be ours. This is its prophetic, soteriological significance. Our sinful nature, in light of the cross and resurrection, can be transfigured into the likeness of Jesus' risen glory: "And we all, with unveiled face, beholding the glory of the Lord, are being changed into his likeness from one degree of glory to another; for this comes from the Lord who is the Spirit" (2 Cor 3:18; cf. 12-17).

While Matthew, Luke, and John have Jesus address his prayer to his Father, only Mark specifies that he used the Aramaic word *Abba*; its only appearance in the Gospels. At this critical juncture, where Jesus experienced both the full burden and stress of his fallen condition and the consummate demand of his filial obedience, Jesus, in addressing his Father as "Abba," acknowledged and professed, despite the appearance of contradictory evidence and feelings, both his Father's intimate love for him and his ardent affection for and loyalty to his Father. "Abba" is an acknowledgment on Jesus' part that the Father does love him. Moreover, "Abba" is the prayer of a loving and obedient Son.[21]

Jesus was so trusting of the Father that, as the loyal Son, he would drink the cup given to him. He would do the Father's will. The significance of Heb 5:7-9 is now apparent:

> In the days of his flesh, Jesus offered up prayers and supplications, with loud cries and tears, to him who was able to save him from death, and he was heard for his godly fear. Although he was a Son, he learned obedience through what he suffered; and being made perfect he became the source of eternal salvation to all who obey him (Heb 5:7-9).

With truly human cries, Jesus called out to the Father. The Father, in turn, heard and answered his prayer because of the reverence and esteem shown to him by his Son. He would not let his holy one see corruption (cf. Acts 2:24-36).

---

[21] This Gethsemane prayer reflects the inner life of the Trinity. "Abba" defines both the Father's eternal relationship (his personhood) to the Son and the Son's relationship (his personhood) to the Father. This "Abba"— the intimate love poured forth from the Father in begetting his Son and uttered back by the Word/Son who is begotten—defines in turn the personhood of the Holy Spirit who proceeds as the mutual "Abba" love from the Father (as source) and the Son, making them one in the Spirit.

Thus in the flesh, within our fallen condition, Jesus learned what it truly means to be a Son of God. Through his suffering—the suffering of temptation, mockery, rejection, hatred, passion, and death—Jesus learned that resolute trust and reverent and devout obedience are the heart of sonship—trust no matter the situation, obedience no matter the cost. Jesus was "faithful over God's house as a son" (Heb 3:6).[22]

In conclusion, we see that we cannot overestimate the significance of Jesus' Gethsemane prayer. It embodied all that Jesus was and interpreted all that he did. In and through this prayer, Jesus owned, in accordance with the Father's will, his and our sinful position with all its overwhelming consequences, and thus seized redemption. The blood of goats and bulls could not save us from sin. But the Father gave to his Son a human nature and it is thus that he declared: "'Lo, I have come to do your will.' And by that will, we have been sanctified through the offering of the body of Jesus Christ once for all" (Heb 10:9-10). The righteousness of the cross, the one obedient act hailed by Paul, sprang from the human will of Jesus, fraught like ours with temptation yet counseled and empowered by the Holy Spirit.

Once again, Scripture is clear that what the Son wills, says, and does as man radically changes the reality of humankind and our relationship to God. Moreover, Jesus' prayer of Gethsemane was clearly the prayer of the cross for there he confirmed and anticipated the offering of his life to his "Abba," Father.

---

[22] The passage could be alluding to Jesus' teaching in the temple at the age of twelve (see Lk 2:41-52).

CHAPTER EIGHT

JESUS: THE CROSS AND RESURRECTION

In returning to the cross and resurrection, we have come full circle in our study. Here, we will limit our examination primarily to some relevant ideas in John's Gospel, especially within the passion narrative, and to the Letter to the Hebrews. While both have distinctive approaches to Jesus' humanity and what he did as man, yet they are strikingly similar to Paul's basic soteriology. Since all are pondering, under the light of the Spirit, the same evidence of faith, this should not be surprising.

It is finished: The Humanity of Jesus in The Gospel of John

The Gospel of John proclaims that the Word who was from the beginning and was with God and was God "became flesh and dwelt among us, full of grace and truth; we have beheld his glory, glory as of the only Son from the Father" (Jn 1:14). Flesh (*sarx*) emphasizes the weakness of Jesus' human condition. (We will examine this more closely in the next chapter.) However, it was within that condition that he manifested the fullness of grace (*charis*) and truth (*aletheia*) (see Jn 1:18). Likewise, it was within the frailty of his humanity that the glory of the only-begotten of the Father was manifested. Jesus' miracles, for example, were signs of his glory. However, we most clearly behold his glory in his filial obedience.

The Obedience of a Son

Jesus' obedience affirmed that he loved the Father as a Son (cf. Jn 14:31): "My food is to do the will of him who sent me, and to accomplish his work" (Jn 4:34; cf. Lk 2:49; Jn 5:30; 6:38). So revealing was his obedience that it manifested his divine Sonship. The Jews accused Jesus of blasphemy because he claimed to be God's Son. Jesus responded: "If I am not doing the works of my Father, then do not believe me; but if I do them, even though you do not believe me, believe the works, that you may know and understand that the Father is in me and I am in the Father" (Jn 10:36-38). The human obedience of Jesus testified to the truth of the Incarnation that indeed the Son of God had assumed our fallen humanity for only a true Son could be so loyal and faithful. The cross became for John the ultimate expression of this truth: "When you have lifted up the Son of man, then you will know that I am he, and that I do nothing on my own authority but speak thus as the Father taught me" (Jn 8:28).[1] The hour of darkness became through obedience the hour of glory.

When I Am Lifted Up

This Johannine image of being lifted up (*hypsoun*) is significant for our study.[2] Jesus said:

No one has ascended into heaven but he who descended from heaven, the Son of man. And as Moses lifted up the

---

[1] The "I Am" specifies the divine name Yahweh. Thus, Jesus was declaring that his true divinity would be manifested in his death on the cross. See R. Brown, *The Gospel According to John,* Vol. I, 533-38.

[2] R. Brown sees in these three passages (3:14; 8:28; 12:32), which speak of Jesus' being lifted up, "the Johannine equivalents of the three predictions of the passion, death, and resurrection found in all the Synoptics (cf. Mk 8:31; 9:31; 10:33-34, and par.)" (*ibid.,* Vol. I, 146).

serpent in the wilderness, so must the Son of man be lifted up [*hypsothenai*], that whoever believes in him may have eternal life. (Jn 3:13-14).

Jesus was referring to the event narrated in Nm 21:4-9 where God, in reaction to the people's having spoken against him, "sent fiery serpents among the people, and they bit the people, so that many people of Israel died." In response to Moses' intercession, God said: "Make a fiery serpent, and set it on a pole; and every one who is bitten, when he sees it, shall live."

Two interrelated questions arise. Firstly, why did God specifically command Moses to lift up an image of what was killing them—a fiery serpent? Why did God not demand that Moses lift up the Ark of the Covenant, his staff, or the stone tablets? They, after all, were signs of God's presence, power, and authority. Secondly, what is the relationship between the fiery serpent which was lifted up and Jesus who will be lifted up?

In directing Moses to lift up the bronze serpent, God was both graphically engraving upon the people's minds the grievous offense they had committed which so provoked such a frightful penalty, and also evoking from them an acknowledgment, in repentance, of their responsibility for such an evil. The bronze serpent was a visible sign convicting them of sin. Their gazing upon it in repentance allowed God to display his merciful healing and deliverance.[3]

---

[3] The book of Wisdom does not see the bronze serpent as directly causing healing, but as a sign of God's healing power: "For he who turned toward it was saved, not by what he saw, but by you, the Savior of all" (Wis 16:7; cf. 16:5-7).

The Israelites preserved in the temple the bronze serpent. They may have done this as a reminder of the consequences of their unfaithfulness and of God's healing mercy. Only during King Hezekiah's reform (716-687 B.C.) was it destroyed for it had become an idol (cf. 1 Kgs 14:4).

When Jesus is lifted up on the cross, what the people and the world will gaze upon is God's graphic depiction of sin, his living fiery serpent. The crucified humanity of Jesus, the *sarx* which bears our sinful human condition, would manifest the outrage of the world's sin (cf. Jn 16:9). So heinous is sin and so awful are its consequences that it caused the Son of God to die on the cross.

The Father will draw all men and women to gaze upon his crucified Son (cf. Jn 6:44). The crucified Jesus himself is equally a magnet drawing all to himself (cf. Jn 12:32). This drawing is an interior evoking of repentance and faith.

Truly to look upon Jesus crucified, to see with the eyes of faith, is to acknowledge in repentance one's sinfulness. Likewise to believe in Jesus, to gaze upon the cross, is to see that he is the "I Am"—the eternal Son of God (cf. Jn 8:28). The author of the Gospel of John, who stood beneath the cross, testified that he looked upon the one who was pierced. This gazing, for John, is to look and perceive in faith who Jesus is (cf. Jn 19:34-

There are similar examples of this type of event in the Old Testament. In Ex 32:20, Moses burned the golden calf, ground it into powder, scattered it "upon the water, and made the people drink it." The drinking of the polluted water forced the people to taste the bitterness of their idolatry and sin. It was thus an act of repentant acknowledgment of evil done, and so formed part of the reconciling process.

Similar practices are found among the ancient Near Eastern peoples. After the Philistines had captured the Ark of the Covenant on the plain of Esdraelon, God inflicted them with tumors (cf. 1 Sm 5:6). The Philistine diviners told the people to send the Ark back, but not empty: "By all means return him [the God of Israel] a guilt offering. Then you will be healed." What was to be the guilt offering? "Five golden tumors and five golden mice, according to the number of the lords of the Philistines; for the same plague was upon all of you and upon your lords" (1 Sm 6:2-4). The golden tumors and mice were acknowledgments of the offense and the just consequences suffered, and thus a means of healing.

37).[4] Only the Son of God could assume our sinful flesh (*sarx*) and, within that flesh, lovingly offer his life to the Father on our behalf. This faith is our healing and eternal life.

Just as the bronze serpent was an incisive depiction of sin and thus a conviction of sin, so too is the lifting up of Jesus. The cross unmasks sin in utter starkness and truth. Likewise, as the bronze serpent was an expression of God's mercy and healing, so too is the cross the ultimate demonstration of the Father's compassion. Christ crucified is the source of eternal life. Jesus' lifeless body is God's icon of sin and love.[5]

Two concluding thoughts on Jesus' being lifted up are appropriate. Firstly, the "lifting up" is not just the exposing of sin depicted in the crucified Jesus. This "lifting up," due to sin, culminates in and is the cause of Jesus' being "lifted up" in the resurrection and ascension. For John, this three-fold "lifting

---

[4] Within the Synoptic tradition, it is the centurion who looks upon the pierced Jesus and proclaims: "Truly this was the Son of God!" (Mt 27:54; cf. Mk 15:39; Lk 23:47).

[5] I have only a layman's acquaintance with the history of Christian art. Yet, I would argue that one of the chief reasons the crucified humanity of Christ, as God's icon of sin and love, was never forsaken within popular Christian piety and devotion is its continual depiction in paintings and crucifixes. Generations of Catholics continue to look upon Jesus lifted up. See Jaroslav Pelikan, *Jesus Through the Centuries: His Place in the History of Culture* (New York: Harper and Row, 1985), 83-94.

This was also aided by the inherited, common, spiritual wisdom, encouraged by the saints, mystics, and spiritual writers, of praying before or holding in one's hand a crucifix. I need to think only of my own Capuchin tradition. The popular pictures (often not very artistic) of Capuchin saints invariably depict them in prayer gazing upon a crucifix held in their hands. This practice cultivated the truth both of our sinfulness and of God's love.

Thus, the present day trend among some to remove crucifixes from churches is an expression (as it was during the iconoclastic controversy) of a docetic or monophysite Christology and of a deficient and defective soteriology.

up" formed one whole integrated process of ascent—a return to the Father—Jesus first and in consequence the rest of us (cf. Jn 6:62; 8:28; 12:32; 20:17; also Acts 2:33; 5:31).

Secondly, in these passages where he spoke of his being lifted up, Jesus consistently referred to himself as "the Son of Man" (cf. Jn 3:13-14; 6:62; 8:28). As the "lifting up" implies both the cross and the glory of the resurrection, so too this title Son of Man embraces both Jesus' solidarity with sinful man and his empowerment by the Father with all honor and authority as the glorious "divine" man who first came down from heaven (cf. Dn 7:13-14). The Son of Man is both the Suffering Servant who takes upon himself our sin and thus, simultaneously, is "exalted and lifted up" (Is 52:13).[6]

Behold the Man

What we have studied thus far is all part of John's use of irony—light in the midst of darkness, glory in weakness, life in death. These function in a way similar to Paul's distinction between flesh and spirit, old creation and new creation. Both sets of antitheses designate and accentuate a transformation, a

---

[6] Jesus' and subsequently the Gospels' use of the title "Son of Man" is a much discussed and debated topic today. The "Son of Man" in the Synoptic tradition falls into three groups: (1) the Son of Man refers to Jesus' earthly ministry (cf. Mk 2:10; Mt 11:19; Lk 7:34; Mt 8:20; Lk 9:58); (2) it is used in relation to his suffering, death, and resurrection (cf. Mk 8:31; 9:31; 10:30); and (3) it refers to his future coming, exaltation, and role in the final judgment (cf. Mk 8:37; 13:24-27; 14:62). For a summary of the contemporary debate, see John Meier, *The New Jerome Biblical Commentary*, 1324-25. See also Marshall, 73-119. The Johannine use of the Son of Man is closely related, as we have already seen, that is, in his being lifted up both on the cross and in his exaltation. Similar then to the Synoptics, though with its unique emphasis, the Gospel of John depicts together the earthly, suffering Son of Man and the exalted, glorious Son of Man. See Francis Moloney, *The New Jerome Biblical Commentary*, 1422-23.

new birth, a re-creation. Thus, these Johannine dichotomies give us a further clue as to John's understanding of Jesus' humanity. The Word became *sarx* and thus lives in "the world" (to use John's term), a world where he experienced darkness, weakness, and death; all of these are the result of sin.[7] Yet Jesus in and through his human weakness brought forth light, truth, and life. John's passion narrative focuses and intensifies these opposing forces testifying to the triumph of the Son.

John's passion narrative begins and ends in a garden (cf. Jn 18:1; 19:41). The darkness of the first garden reminds us of the Garden of Eden where sin brought darkness and death into the world. No longer did the light of truth shine. Jesus was now in the midst of this garden of darkness (the world) and, as one like ourselves, he confronted the accumulated evil of the centuries personified in Judas. For John, Jesus was the light shining in the darkness which could not overcome him (Jn 1:50).[8] Through his passion and death (the hour of darkness), Jesus would transform the garden of darkness and evil (the world) into a garden of resurrected light and life (a new world).

In typical Johannine irony, the soldiers hailed the scourged, beaten, crowned, and humiliated Jesus as the king of the Jews.[9]

---

[7] The term "world" construed theologically in John has the meaning of those hostile to God, Jesus, and his disciples (see Jn 1:9-10; 7:7; 15:18-19; 17:14). The world in this sense is the domain of Satan (cf. Jn 12:31; 14:30; 16:11; 1 Jn 5:19).

[8] Unlike the Synoptics, John's Gospel has the Jews and soldiers carrying lanterns when they come to arrest Jesus. While they are in the presence of the "light of the world," they are in darkness and thus in need of artificial light. See I. de la Potterie, *The Hour of Jesus* (New York: Alba House, 1989), 28.

[9] In contrast to Matthew and Mark, John understates the humiliation of Jesus. He does not speak of the soldiers striking or spitting upon Jesus (cf. Mt 27:28-31; Mk 15:17-20). John does not wish to deny the reality of Jesus' suffering. Rather his interest is to verify that in the midst of this suffering, the glory of Jesus was disclosed.

Contrary to the Synoptic accounts, Pilate brought Jesus out before the crowd wearing the crown of thorns and dressed in royal purple. Pilate declared: "Behold the man!" (Jn 19:5). As we noted earlier in relationship to "the lifting up of the Son of Man," John seems to see in the emphasis "*the* man" an inference both to the Suffering Servant of Is 53:3-4 (a man of sorrows, and acquainted with grief, one stricken, smitten, and afflicted) and to the "Son of Man" of Daniel, one who would receive from God an everlasting kingdom in which people of all nations and languages would serve him (cf. Dn 7:13-14; Zec 6:9-14). These contrasting images focused on one and the same man are exactly what John wishes us to perceive. The one who bears our sin is our king. The glory of Jesus was manifested and the transformation of the world was achieved through his grotesque humanity, "as one from whom men hide their faces" (Is 53:3).

"Knowing that all was now finished, [Jesus] said…, 'I thirst'" (Jn 19:28; cf. Pss 22:15 and 69:21). Jesus surely had been physically thirsty. For three hours, his body had been writhing and racked in pain. For John, though, this physical thirst revealed a deeper thirst. Jesus himself, experiencing the full weight of our sinful condition, anguished for new life: "Father, the hour has come; glorify your Son that the Son may glorify you." Simultaneously he deeply longed for the salvation of all—"since you [Father] have given him [the Son] power over all flesh, to give eternal life to all whom you have given him" (Jn 17:1-2). The irony for John is that the one who in the flesh was thirsting is the very one who would quench the thirst of those who were parched (those also in the flesh). He would give the living water of the Holy Spirit.

This recalls Jesus' meeting at the well with the Samaritan woman. He was thirsty then also (an effect of sin), and yet he promised that he would give living water (cf. Jn 4:7-15). Later in Jerusalem, Jesus proclaimed, "If anyone is thirsty, let him come to me and drink. He who believes in me, as the scripture has said, 'Out of his heart shall flow rivers of living water.'" John editorialized: "Now this he said about the Spirit, which those who believed in him were to receive, for as yet the Spirit had not been given, because Jesus was not yet glorified" (Jn 7:37-38).

Gave up His Spirit

Here on the cross, the hour of Jesus' glory had arrived. Now he was empowered to pour out his Spirit upon the world. In reparation for sin, he had offered up his holy, innocent life on our behalf. He could truly say: "It is finished." John concluded: "He bowed his head and gave up his spirit" (Jn 19:30).

As with Paul, this moment is the most decisive in all of history. At the moment when sin and death appeared to have triumphed—the old creation was fully displayed in Jesus' crucified body—Jesus vanquished both.

Firstly, notice that Jesus' death was not passive. *He* concluded that his work was done. *He* bowed his head (his head did not slump because of death) and *he* freely gave up his spirit (death did not rob him of his spirit) (Jn 10:18). Thus, even more graphically than in Paul, we see that, on the cross, Jesus actively and purposely put our flesh (*sarx*) to death. It was due to his human will and action.

Secondly, John (or someone of his school) coined the Greek phrase "he gave forth his spirit" (*kai klinas ten kethalen paredoken to pneuma*). Nowhere in antiquity is death described as the giving forth of one's spirit.[10] The same breath by which our sinful flesh was put to death was equally the very same breath (life) offered to the Father in reparation for sin, and so the same breath by which the Holy Spirit was poured out upon

---

[10] See I. de la Potterie, *The Hour of Jesus*, 131-33.

the world. For John, the last agonizing breath of Jesus, a life handed over in love to the Father, was the first breath of new and eternal life for humanity. In the death of Jesus, the end and beginning are the same—ultimate glory and life displayed in utter weakness.

Thus Jesus' words, "It is finished," have a three-fold meaning. With the obedient conclusion of his Father's work, Jesus ended the old creation and completed the new creation. All was finished and Jesus could now take his Sabbath rest (cf. Gn 2:1-3; Heb 4).

Blood and Water

Since Jesus was already dead, the soldiers did not break his legs. However, one of the soldiers pierced his side and "at once there came out blood and water" (Jn 19:32-35).

Not having his bones broken confirmed that Jesus was the new paschal lamb (see Ex 12:46). Moreover, Jesus died at the hour when the paschal lambs were being sacrificed in the Temple. Having assumed our sinful condition, Jesus then is the true Lamb of God who takes away the sin of the world (see Jn 1:36).

The blood and water that flowed from the side of Jesus represent both cleansing and life. There is a reciprocal causal relationship between them. The outpouring of the Spirit of life is the first direct consequence of the cleansing of sin in the blood of Jesus (cf. 1 Jn 1:7). Having reconciled us to the Father in the offering of his life (through his blood—cf. Lv 17:11,14), he enabled us to share in his Spirit of Sonship. Through the blood of Jesus, we have access to the Spirit of life. In turn, to those who believe, the Spirit makes present the cleansing power of Jesus' blood shed on the cross.

Moreover, for John, the blood and water that flowed from the side of Jesus were a prophetic sign that his sacrifice on the cross was acceptable to God the Father. The life-giving water of the Holy Spirit testified and certified that his blood (the offering of his life) had made reparation and atonement for the sins committed against the love and holiness of God the Father. The Father manifested the superabundant worth of his Son's sacrifice, the offering of his life in love, in the outpouring of the Holy Spirit.

Receive the Holy Spirit

On the first Easter evening, according to John, Jesus appeared to his disciples. What transpired is a resurrection account and interpretation of what happened on the cross. It is an Easter view of the cross.

Jesus stood among them and said:

> "Peace be with you." When he had said this, he showed them his hands and his side. Then the disciples were glad when they saw the Lord. Jesus said to them again, "Peace be with you. As the Father has sent me, even so I send you." And when he had said this, he breathed on them, and said to them, "Receive the Holy Spirit. If you forgive the sins of any, they are forgiven; if you retain the sins of any, they are retained". (Jn 20:19-23).

Firstly, Jesus twice greeted the disciples with the words, "Peace be with you" as he displayed the marks in his hands and side (see also Jn 20:26). Peace is the immediate consequence of Jesus' death, the fruit of his crucified body. Through his death, Jesus reconciled us to the Father, making peace through the blood of his cross (cf. 1 Jn 2:2; 4:10; Col 1:20). To Mary Magdalene, Jesus said: "Go to my brethren and say to them, I am ascending to my Father and your Father, to my God and to your God" (Jn 20:17).

Secondly, the nail and spear marks, still visible in Jesus' glorified body, testified both to his former condition, a man under the curse of sin, and to his triumph over sin within that condition. The stigma of sin has been transfigured into the stigmata of glory.

Thirdly, Jesus breathed upon his disciples, conferring upon them the life of the Holy Spirit. In so doing, he gave them authority to forgive sin. This is the Johannine Pentecost and it is reminiscent of both the second creation story and Jesus' breathing forth his Spirit on the cross.

In the second creation story, God created man by breathing into him his very own spirit (Gn 2:7). We lost this spirit of life through sin. Now Jesus, as the risen Lord, stands in the place of Yahweh and re-creates us by once more breathing into us the same Holy Spirit, which is the first and foremost fruit of the cross (cf. Jn 19:30). Similar to Pauline soteriology, John recognizes that what is born of the flesh is flesh and what is born of the Spirit is Spirit (cf. Jn 3:1-6).

For John, in conclusion, earth is for Jesus and can be for us a mirror reflection of heaven. In heaven, the Son, for all eternity, is the loyal, faithful, loving, and obedient Son of the Father from whom he receives all. This is why he is the Son. The Father eternally loves the Son he begets, lavishing upon him all glory and honor. This is why he is the Father. On earth, under the most adverse conditions, this eternal drama of mutual love and honor has now been played out in time. What our study of John has shown is that in and through this earthly liturgy, Jesus, as truly one of us, has made it possible for us to be assumed into this eternal drama of mutual love and honor, becoming adopted sons and daughters, born of the Spirit, and thus sharing in the glory the Father gave Jesus.

Tasting Death for Us: The Humanity of Jesus in the Letter to the Hebrews

The Letter to the Hebrews is explicitly and integrally entwined with the Old Testament. Written within a Hebrew\Hellenistic milieu (possibly at Alexandria), its proposition is that in his sacrifice, Jesus' fulfilled, superseded, and surpassed the old covenant.[11]

The paramount truth is that Jesus is now the glorious, risen, incarnate Son (Heb 1). All that Jesus was and did on earth is interpreted in light of his present heavenly existence. The author of Hebrews, gazing upon the historical and earthly work of Jesus from the heights of heaven, recognizes that such a perspective does not diminish what Jesus did, but rather enhances his accomplishments and causes us to revere even more "such a great salvation" (Heb 2:3).

The Letter to the Hebrews acknowledges that Jesus is the Son who took on a humanity from our common, sinful stock and that, like us, he was tempted in every way though without personal sin (cf. Heb 1:2; 2:11,14,17-18; 4:15). (We will examine this more closely in the following chapter on the Incarnation.) His human obedience to the Father, in the midst of intense suffering and trust, taught him the meaning of Sonship and was the cause of his being exalted as our eternal high priest (Heb 5:7-10). In and through his human life, he was perfected.

As with Paul and John, the author of the Letter to the Hebrews sees the death of Jesus both as the place where his identity with our sinful condition is most clearly experienced, and as the definitive justification for his glorification and our salvation. Here, then, we will examine the Letter to the Hebrews' theology of the cross.

Tasting Death for Everyone

The height to which Jesus is now exalted corresponds to the depth of his ignominy: "We see Jesus, who for a little while was

---

[11] See Philip Edgecumbe Hughes, *A Commentary on the Epistle to the Hebrews* (Grand Rapids, MI: Eerdmans, 1977), 1-32.

made lower than the angels, crowned with glory and honor because of the suffering of death, so that by the grace of God he might taste death for everyone" (Heb 2:8-9). Having assumed our human condition, Jesus in truth could die. But the passage goes further and states that Jesus tasted death for everyone (*uper pantos geusetai thanatou*). This is unique to this letter, and important for our study.

Death, as we know it, is a result of sin (cf. Gn 2:17). It is a physical sign of our being separated from the living God. Thus to experience the full reality of death means that a person not only dies physically, but also endures absolute alienation from God. This is the "natural" consequence or punishment for sin.

As a man, within our fallen condition, Jesus experienced for us, that we might be spared, the full weight of sin and death— estrangement from his Father. He personally endured the full horror of our punishment. This interpretation is confirmed if we take into account the alternate reading found in some ancient manuscripts: "*so that apart from God [choris theou]* he [Jesus] tasted death for us."[12] This passage testifies to the truth that it was our fallen nature that Jesus assumed with all its consequences. No wonder Jesus' Gethsemane prayer was so anguished for it was the cup of death in its fullness that he was willing to drink. Only by experiencing the fullness of death, however, could he put the whole of death to death. In accordance with our soteriological principle, if Jesus had not assumed the fullness of our death, we would not have been saved from it. It would still be ours.[13]

Moreover, this insight gives new depth of meaning to Jesus' prayerful cry from the cross: "My God, my God, why have you forsaken me?" (Mt 27:46; cf. Mk 15:34). His prayer was not

---

[12] *Ibid.*, 87-97

[13] For von Balthasar's theology of Holy Saturday concerning Jesus' descent into hell, see *Mysterium Paschale*, 148-88.

a cry of despair, but of hope: "In the days of his flesh, Jesus offered up prayers and supplications, with loud cries and tears, to him who was able to save him from death, and he was heard for his godly fear" (Heb 5:7). In praying Ps 22, Jesus not only expressed the intensity of his human experience of sin (alienation from God), but also, as the ever faithful Son, prayed in hope and trust:

> But you, O Lord, be not far off! O you my help, hasten to my aid! Deliver my soul from the sword, my life from the power of the dog! Save me from the mouth of the lion, my afflicted soul from the horns of the wild oxen. . . . For he [God] has not despised or abhorred the affliction of the afflicted; and he has not hid his face from him, but has heard, when he cried to him. (Ps 22:19-21,24).

Notice then that Jesus only tasted death for us. While he endured separation from his Father, it was not a permanent state. Although Jesus willingly and obediently suffered the full weight of sin on our behalf, the Father would not allow his holy Son to languish in hell. He raised him up.

Opening Through the Curtain

Jesus is now the eternal high priest crowned in glory not only because he tasted death, but also because he simultaneously offered his holy and innocent life to the Father on our behalf. Unlike the blood of goats and bulls offered in an earthly temple, Jesus entered the heavenly temple "with his own blood, thus securing an eternal redemption" (Heb 9:12). Jesus' offering of his life, his blood, was a thoroughly human, free act performed in union with the Holy Spirit so that we might be purified of sin and now confidently enter once more the heavenly sanctuary of God with the full assurance of faith (cf. Heb 9:12-15,24-28; 10:4-10).

We once again perceive that this "new and living way" to the Father is through the humanity of the Son. The barrier of sin, symbolized by the curtain in the temple, which kept us from the Holy of Holies, that is, from the full presence of God, was opened through the humanity of Jesus (cf. Heb 9:6-10; Lv 16; Is 6:1-7). More so, his humanity is the opening itself. We can enter into the heavenly temple "which he [Jesus] opened for us through the curtain, that is, through his flesh" (Heb 10:20).

If the curtain in the temple symbolizes Jesus' flesh, then the curtain also testifies to the fallenness of his humanity for the curtain is a testimony to sin. However, our opening to God is through that flesh, that curtain, for in and through the offering of Jesus' obedient and holy life to the Father, the flesh of sin, the curtain, is pierced.[14] Because of the precious offering of his innocent blood, we now have "a high priest, holy, blameless, unstained, separated from sinners, exalted above the heavens" (Heb 7:26).

Consciences Purified

As with Paul and John, the author of Hebrews recognized, within his own context and theology, that what Jesus did as one of us substantially changed us and our relationship to God. He did more than make a good situation better. What the old covenant and the old priesthood could not do is now accomplished. Our consciences are purified of dead works, that is, we are freed of the guilt, shame, and condemnation accrued through sin (Heb 9:14). Our hearts are sprinkled clean and our bodies washed in the pure water of the Spirit (Heb 10:22). All of this is predicated upon "Jesus, the mediator of a new covenant, and to the sprinkled blood that speaks more graciously than the blood of Abel" (Heb 12:24).

---

[14] This is similar to Paul's notion of the circumcision of Jesus' flesh. Cf. Col 2:11-12.

Thus the argument advanced in the Letter to Hebrews is fundamentally eschatological. Jesus, who belonged to our sinful stock, has enacted a better covenant with better promises (Heb 8:6). We should never neglect so great a salvation (Heb 2:3). Neither our faith nor our hope must falter (Heb 11:1). We must "hold fast the confession of our hope without wavering, for he who promised is faithful" (Heb 10:23; cf. 10:36,39). The heavenly Jesus is our forerunner, our sure hope, the anchor behind the curtain (cf. 6:19).

Christians are to anticipate that day when all will be subjected to Christ (Heb 2:8). Already he is "seated at the right hand of the throne of God" (Heb 12:2). He is the high priest "by the power of an indestructible life" (Heb 7:16). The perfection of Jesus is to be ours on the day of his coming, for we also possess that same heavenly call to glory (Heb 2:10; 3:1). He will perfect "for all times those who are sanctified" (Heb 10:14, cf. 10:2; 11:40). For in Christ and through his blood, we can approach "Mount Zion and the city of living God, the heavenly Jerusalem" (Heb 12:22-24).

Now we must eagerly wait to "receive the promised eternal inheritance" (Heb 9:15; cf. 9:28). "For here we have no lasting city, but we seek the city which is to come" (Heb 13:14). Through obedience to God's commands, we strive to enter into his eternal sabbath rest (Heb 4:11). In the face of trials and persecutions, we must look to Jesus "the pioneer and perfecter of our faith" (Heb 12:2). The discipline we endure is so that we might forever "share his [God's] holiness" (Heb 12:10).

The Letter to the Hebrews voices an ardent and realistic expectancy of Jesus' coming. There is an unwavering and steadfast assurance that the moment of his coming will actually arrive. This staunch faith and firm hope are founded upon the truth that the Son entered into our human sinful condition and as one of us offered his life to the Father. This offering not only perfected Jesus, but also is the assurance of our own eternal perfection.

CHAPTER NINE

THE INCARNATION: THE WORD BECAME FLESH

The New Testament teaching which we have examined on the "sinful" humanity of Jesus converges now on the question of the Incarnation. Not only did the early Christians come to believe that Jesus was the eternal Son of God, but also that this divine Son in becoming man took on our sinful condition. It may not be accidental that the later high Christology of the infancy narratives, the Johannine corpus, and the Letter to the Hebrews not only clearly proclaim the divinity of Jesus, but also provide some of the clearest teaching concerning Jesus' human condition, that he was of Adam's stock.[1] From what we

---

[1] While we have referred to high Christology as later, we do not imply that it was in any sense less authentic than what came before it. Scripture scholars and theologians debate the nature and sequences of New Testament christological development (see R. Brown, *Biblical Reflections on Crises Facing the Church* (New York: Paulist Press, 1975), 20-37; O. Cullmann, *The Christology of the New Testament* (Philadelphia: Westminster Press, 1958); James D.G. Dunn, *Christology in the Making* (Philadelphia: Westminster Press, 1980); R. Fuller, *The Foundations of New Testament Christology* (New York: Charles Scribner's Sons, 1965); I. Howard Marshall, *The Origins of New Testament Christology* (Downers Grove, IL: InterVarsity Press, 1976); C.F.D. Moule, *The Origin of Christology* (Cambridge: University Press, 1977); William M. Thompson, *The Jesus Debate* (New York: Paulist Press, 1985). Nonetheless, even at the earliest strata of the New Testament proclamation, there is clear evidence that Jesus

have already learned, we can conceive how the faith of the early Church may have developed.

Jesus' followers and disciples witnessed and the early Christians remembered that he associated closely with sinners. For example, having called Levi, a tax collector, to be his disciple, Jesus went to his house to eat:

> And as he sat at table in his house, many tax collectors and sinners were sitting with Jesus and his disciples; for there were many who followed him. And the scribes of the Pharisees, when they saw that he was eating with sinners and tax collectors, said to his disciples, "Why does he eat with tax collectors and sinners?" And when Jesus heard it, he said to them, "Those who are well have no need of a physician, but those who are sick; I came not to call the righteous, but sinners." (Mk 2:15-17. See Mt 9:9-13; Lk 5:27-32).

This solidarity with sinners became the hallmark of Jesus' ministry.[2] While it scandalized the self-righteous, it forthrightly manifested that Jesus did not set himself apart from us, but rather truly was one with our sinful condition. He became so precisely to be our physician, our healer.

Moreover, the early Church perceived just how intimately Jesus had affiliated himself with our sinfulness when they saw him crucified in the midst of thieves. According to the Gospel of Luke, Jesus had foretold: "For I tell you that this scripture must be fulfilled in me, 'And he was reckoned with transgressors'; for what is written about me has its fulfillment" (Lk

---

revealed himself to be divine and thus founded the early Church's belief in his divinity. See, for example, I. Howard Marshall, *Jesus the Savior: Studies in New Testament Theology*, 134-210; G. O'Collins, *Interpreting Jesus*.

[2] Jesus' table fellowship with sinners would have rendered him ritually impure.

22:37; see Is 53:12).[3] On the cross, Jesus revealed that he was the Suffering Servant who bore our sinful flesh with its punishment.

Thus through the testimony of Jesus' life and death, his followers recognized in faith that he took upon himself our sinful state and thus comprehended more fully that this solidarity was not first achieved in his passion and death, or during his public ministry, or even at his baptism. Rather, they perceived that the reason Jesus identified with our sinful condition at his baptism, associated and ate with sinners during his ministry, and died a sinner's death, all to the scandal of the self-righteous, was that he was actually born as one of us, as part of the sinful race of Adam.

We want to examine now how the New Testament bears witness to this truth in its proclamation of the Incarnation.

Jesus' Ancestry

The infancy narratives are more subtle than the Pauline writings concerning the specific nature of Jesus' humanity, but the insight into his ancestry is found within both groups of writings. Jesus was a "son of David, the son of Abraham" (Mt 1:1). In Luke, Jesus' ancestry is traced to Adam (cf. Lk 3:23-37). Jesus' ancestors were more than common sinners; they were often a despicable lot. Far from hiding this fact, the Gospel writers appear to glory in it. It was from these ancestors

---

[3] The Gospel of Mark specifies that Jesus was crucified between two robbers. While the earliest and best manuscripts do not have what came to be the next verse, later manuscripts added, more than likely from the Gospel of Luke, "And the scripture was fulfilled which says, 'he was reckoned with the transgressors'" (Mk 15:27-28).

that Jesus took his flesh. He was one of them, and thus he was deeply woven within the defiled but common fabric of man.[4]

Moreover, while Jesus was conceived of the Holy Spirit and would be known as "Son of the Most High" and be "called holy," yet within human history (riddled with sin and injustice), he was registered, according to the Gospel of Luke, in Augustus' census; thus, numbered as one among us for it was our flesh that he bore (Lk 2:1-7).

What we discern here is the consummation of the whole Old Testament revelation. While the God of Abraham, Isaac, and Jacob revealed himself to be the all-holy God, entirely transcending the milieu of sin and evil, yet from the time of the patriarchs, he consistently entangled himself with fallen man and immersed himself thoroughly in man's sinful history. He did not stand aloof. He manifested, in word and deed, that he is the Holy One in our (sinful) midst (cf. Hos 11:9; Am 4:2).

The Sinai covenant best illustrates that God related to and dwelt among his sinful people. Despite the Israelites' idolatrous worship of the golden calf, God nonetheless made a covenant with them: "The LORD, the LORD, a God merciful and gracious, slow to anger, and abounding in steadfast love and faithfulness, keeping steadfast love for thousands, forgiving iniquity and transgression and sin" (Ex 34:6-7; cf. 32-34). By dirtying his hands in real history and in genuine human life, God labored to make his people holy.[5]

---

[4] See Francis Wright Beare, *The Gospel According to Matthew* (San Francisco: Harper and Row, 1981), 61-65. See also Joseph Fitzmyer, *The Gospel According to Luke*, Vol. 1 (The Anchor Bible, 28) (New York: Doubleday, 1981), 488-505; Benedict Viviano, *The New Jerome Biblical Commentary*, 634-35; Robert Karris, *The New Jerome Biblical Commentary*, 687-88.

[5] There are multiple examples in the Old Testament of God's involving himself in the lives of sinful men and sinful situations. The lives of the patriarchs—Abraham, Isaac, Jacob, and Joseph—as well as the jaded

With Jesus, this *kenosis*—God's going out of himself and emptying himself into our sinful condition—finds its completion and fullest expression. In assuming our fallen humanity, God literally toiled unto death, with human outstretched hands, in the filth of human sin.

The Word Became Flesh

John's Gospel clearly recognizes this foundational principle of divine revelation and conclusively testifies to its truth. John emphasizes, possibly in response to Gnosticism and Docetism, that the Word did not just become *soma*, that is, take upon himself a generic human body and life, but rather became *sarx*, that is, took on flesh in all its human frailty and weakness, which are the consequences of sin (Jn 1:14; cf. 1 Jn 4:2-3; 2 Jn 7).[6]

John's Gospel also recalls the Old Testament image of God's dwelling in the midst of his sinful people (see Jn 1:14). Leviticus 26:11 states: "I will make my abode among you, and my soul shall not abhor you" (cf. Ex 25:8; Dt 4:7; 1 Kgs 8:25-27). As God in his sanctuary dwelt among the ungodly, so now in the new temple of his flesh (tainted by sin, but being made holy), the Son of God abided with unrighteous humanity (cf. Jn 2:18-22; Sir 24).

While John tends occasionally to diminish the suffering and humiliation of Jesus (we saw this in the passion narrative) and to give him a hallowed demeanor (evident in the manner and style of his speech), yet he does not lose the significance of

history of the kings—Saul, David, and Solomon—testify that God did not remove himself from the sinful circumstances that beset them or even from their corrupt deeds.

6. See R. Brown, *The Gospel According to John,* Vol. 1 (The Anchor Bible, 29), 30-35. First Jn 4:2-3 declares that the antichrist is precisely the person who does not confess that Jesus Christ "has come in the flesh" (*en sarki*).

Jesus' being human, but underscores that only in and through this flawed humanity (*sarx*) is the glory of the only-begotten Son manifested: ". . .and we have seen his glory [*doxa*, or *shekinah* in the Hebrew Scriptures], glory as of the only Son from the Father" (Jn 1:14; cf. Ex 25:8; 40:34). *Sarx* alone radiates and mirrors *doxa*. Thus, loyal to the truth of the Incarnation that the Word actually became flesh, the Gospel of John portrays the divine personhood of Jesus brilliantly shining in and through the words and actions of a man like ourselves.

Of the Same Stock

Lastly, the Letter to the Hebrews, referring to the Incarnation, declares that Jesus was "made a little lower than the angels" (Heb 2:9). He who made all things is also the "pioneer" of our salvation, not shrinking from the cross (cf. Heb 12:2). "For he who sanctifies and those who are sanctified have all one origin [are of the same stock—*ek evos pantes*, literally, out of one all]" (Heb 2:11). What is the one stock from which Jesus obtained our sanctification and from which we are sanctified?

> Since therefore the children share in flesh and blood, he himself likewise partook of the same nature [*meteschen ton auton*, literally: he shared the same things] that through death he might destroy him who has the power of death, that is the devil, and deliver all those who through fear of death were subject to lifelong bondage. (Heb 2:14-15).

One could interpret this passage in a generic sense—the Son became a man (same nature) untouched by the effects of sin. However, the argument in the text runs contrary to this. Jesus shared in the very same things we did. Our flesh and blood were under the power of the devil and the fear of death—due to sin—and it was from this stock that Jesus acquired his flesh and blood. Thus he became, by means of this disfigured humanity, our deliverer and the pioneer of our freedom and life.[7]

We now perceive why the Letter to the Hebrews states that Jesus disregarded the embarrassment of our fellowship. Only if Jesus partook of everyone's sinful condition would it make sense to declare that he was "not ashamed to call them brethren" (Heb 2:11). Jesus disregarded the shame of our condition in assuming our sinful stock and belonging to our unrighteous fraternity. As a true brother, Jesus lived as we do and placed his trust, as we should, in God (cf. Heb 2:12-13).

Moreover, we also find in the Letter to the Hebrews an incarnational insight that was also prevalent for Paul's and John's theology of the cross, that is, Jesus' human obedience. The Letter, quoting Psalm 40, dramatizes this truth:

> When Christ came into the world, he said, "Sacrifices and offerings you have not desired, but a body have you prepared for me; in burnt offerings and sin offerings you have taken no pleasure. Then I said, 'Lo, I have come to do your will, O God,' as it is written of me in the roll of the book."....And by that will we have been sanctified through the offering of the body of Jesus Christ once for all. (Heb 10:5-10).

We see parallels in this passage, the second building upon the first and together accenting the supremacy of the Incarnation and the cross over the Old Testament prefigurements:

---

[7] In an excellent study on the priesthood of Jesus, Vanhoye shows that unlike the priests of the Old Testament, who were to be physically perfect and ritually pure and thus worthy to enter into the presence of God, Jesus identified with our sinful condition. Only in such a condition could he, as one of us on our behalf, offer his holy life to God. See A. Vanhoye, *Old Testament Priests and the New Priest* (Petersham: St. Bede's Publications, 1986) 73, 80, 87, 112-20, 130, 132.

1. Sacrifices and offerings   a body have you
   you have not desired   prepared for me
2. In sin offerings you have   'Lo, I have come to do
   taken no pleasure   your will, O God'

In contrast to the spurned sacrifices and offerings of the Old Testament, God gave to Jesus a "body" in which he would offer himself to the Father. Similarly, in the past, sin offerings gave no pleasure to God, but now within that "body," that is, as a man, Jesus offered the Father a pleasing sacrifice for, unlike the bulls and goats of old, this offering was done freely in obedience to God: "Lo, I have come to do your will." We have been sanctified by this human will for, in and through this will, the Son freely offered up his human life (of our fallen stock yet without sin) to the Father.

This passage illustrates the intrinsic affinity, evident throughout the whole of Hebrews, between the Incarnation and the cross. Only because the Father gave to the Son a "body" like our own could the Son, in turn, freely offer to the Father his holy and righteous life as a sin offering. The Incarnation itself then must presuppose and intimate the cross, containing within it the seeds of the cross, and it can do so only if the humanity Jesus assumed is of our sinful stock.

In this light, too, we can grasp the significance of the perfecting of Jesus. The Letter to the Hebrews states that it is fitting that God should make "perfect through suffering" the pioneer of our salvation, thus bringing many sons to glory (Heb 2:10). As Son of God, Jesus is eternally perfect. However, since Jesus shared in our imperfection (our sinful stock), "beset with weakness" (Heb 5:2), he too had to be brought to perfection. Bearing the birthmark of sin and death, Jesus' humanity was also in need of redemption (cf. Heb 2:10) This perfection or transformation was achieved through the offering up of his blood on the cross "by which he was sanctified"

(Heb 10:29). In raising Jesus from the dead, the Father appointed him to be the eternal High Priest, "a Son who has been made perfect for ever" (Heb 7:28).[8]

Similar to Pauline soteriology, the Letter to the Hebrews sees this transformation as the prerequisite of our own. While the old sacrifices could not make us perfect (see Heb 10:1), the single sacrifice of Jesus, by which he himself has been per- fected, "has perfected for all time those who are sanctified" (Heb 10:14; cf. 12:23). Jesus assumed our imperfect humanity and in so doing, perfected it on the cross. Christians, in this life, are coming to perfection in Christ and in heaven will join "the spirits of just men made perfect" (Heb 12:23).

****

We have seen that the New Testament testifies that in every aspect of his life, from his conception to his death, Jesus lived fully within our human condition, a human life that had been marred and tainted by sin. He bore the sinful birthmark of Adam. Before we draw our final conclusions, we will examine one final facet of Christology—the primacy of Christ.

---

[8] See Vanhoye, 83, 130-33, 118-20.

CHAPTER 10

THE SINFUL HUMANITY OF JESUS AND THE PRIMACY OF CHRIST

In concluding our study we must examine the relationship between the sinful humanity of Jesus and the primacy of Christ. They form a unity that cannot be broken because God the Father has himself joined them together.

Since the fourteenth century, two schools of theological thought — the Franciscan and the Dominican — along with their respective sympathizers have engaged in a protracted debate over the rationale for the Incarnation. The Dominicans, following their esteemed brother St Thomas Aquinas (1225-1274), advocate the theory that the Incarnation was primarily for the salvation of fallen humanity. If mankind had not sinned, Jesus would not have become man.[1] Inspired by

---

[1]Actually, Aquinas gave a rather guarded answer to the proposed question. In his commentary on *The Sentences* of Peter Lombard, he stated that he favored the opinion that the Son would not have become man if man had not sinned since this answer has the authority of Scripture and tradition. However, he acknowledged that because the exaltation of human nature and the consummation of the universe are achieved through the Incarnation the other opinion can also be called probable. Cf. *In III Sententiae*, d.1,1,3. In his commentary on The First Letter to Timothy, he similarly argued that we cannot be certain of what God might have done under different circumstances. However, what we do know is that Scripture tells us that the Son became man because of sin. See *In 1 Timothius*, c. 1, lect. 4; also *De Veritate* 29, 4, 3. In the *Summa Theologica*, he likewise

their confrere, John Duns Scotus (1265-1308), the Franciscans, on the other hand, champion the view that since God the Father created everything for Christ, the Son of God would have become man rightfully to claim his kingdom, regardless of humanity's fall. The primacy of Christ alone demanded the Incarnation.[2]

Aquinas aptly sees that the question traditionally formulated is hypothetical (and so misplaced) and thus cannot be answered with certainty. How can we possibly know with assurance whether or not the Son would have become man if we had not sinned? However, the concern over the primacy of Christ is not lost with the displacing of this hypothetical question. The substantive issue is whether or not God the Father desired to manifest the glory of his Son and to do so as a man. The answer to this question has significance not only for the status of Jesus, but also for our own self-understanding as human beings. Were we created for our own glory or were we created for the glory of Jesus, a glory that we ourselves

---

appealed to the authority of Scripture. See *Summa Theologica*, III, 1, 3. For a discussion of these texts see J. Carol, *Why Jesus Christ?: Thomistic, Scotistic and Conciliatory Perspectives* (Manassas: Trinity Communicatons, 1986), 8-22. See also T. R. Potvin, *The Theology of the Primacy of Christ According to St Thomas and its Scriptural Foundations* (Studia Friburgensia: New Series, 50) (Fribourg, Switzerland: University Press, 1973).

[2]Duns Scotus argued that the end for which God creates human beings (their predestination) is for their glory. Within this end he predestined the soul (humanity) of Christ to possess the greatest glory and thus he has primacy of place within God's plan. Sin enters in only as a secondary concern and as an obstacle to this end. Thus, the Son would have become man regardless of sin because the primary end of creation is the glorification of the soul of Christ and of all human beings. Cf. *Ordinatio*, III, 7, 3 and III, 19; *Opus Parisiense*, III, 7, 4; *Reportatio Trencensis*, III, 7, 4; *Lectura Completa*, III, 7, 3; *Reportatio Barcinonesis*, II, 7, 3. For a discussion of these texts see Carol, pp. 121-49.

would share in, but only secondarily? We suggest that we were created, in accordance with the Father's will, to witness the glory of Jesus and to praise him eternally for his glory. Accordingly, the Incarnation takes logical precedence within the Father's eternal pre-ordained will. However, Jesus' primacy, the reason for his pre-eminence, is fully manifested only within the world as it is. Thus the glory of the Incarnate Son was definitively demonstrated only within his sinful humanity and was thoroughly confirmed only in the redemptive work he performed under the conditions of sin. Only as redeemed human beings, then, are we empowered to praise his glory.[3] This understanding supplants the misdirected conflict between the Scotists and Thomists and gives to the whole issue a more true-to-life and true-to-history perspective.[4]

The Colossian Hymn: Pre-eminent in Every Way

The author of Colossians (probably not Paul) wrote to the Christians of Colossae because he was concerned with their flirting with empty philosophies and "the elemental spirits of the universe" and not remaining loyal to the Gospel "according to Christ" (Col. 2:8). Contrary to possibly gnostic teaching, only in Jesus does "the whole fullness of deity dwell bodily" (Col. 2:9). Thus Paul asserted in no uncertain terms the pre-eminence of Christ.

---

[3]Within this perspective, sin can be defined as robbing Jesus of his rightful glory and so usurping his primacy of place. Allegorically we see this in the Fall. Adam and Eve ate from the tree of the knowledge of good and evil (they would be gods and hold pride of place) rather than from the tree of life, which in light of the cross, represents Jesus (cf. Gn 3). In John's Gospel, the primordial sin is not to believe in and thus not to give glory to the one sent by the Father (cf. Jn 8:22-24; 15:22; 16:9).

[4]For the history of the debate including all the relevant patristic, medieval, and modern texts, plus pertinent ecclesial statements and documents, see Carol, *Why Jesus Christ?*.

The early Christian hymn, found in the Letter to the Colossians, which was Duns Scotus' theological inspiration (see Col. 1:15-20; cf. Eph 1:10, 20-23; Heb. 1:1-4), must be interpreted in this context.[5] This hymn proclaims what is now referred to, following Scotus, as the primacy of Christ. This liturgical hymn can be divided into two stanzas (vs. 15-17 and 18-20).[6]

The first stanza proclaims that Jesus, the incarnate Son, is "the image of the invisible God". He is "firstborn of all creation" — not in time, but in the Father's mind. All was created "in him" — "things visible and invisible, whether thrones or dominions, or principalities or authorities — all were created by and for him [*eis auton*]. He is before all things, and in him all things hold together" (Col. 1:15-17, cf. Heb. 1:3, 6, Jn. 1:3, 18). Why is Jesus the centerpiece of the Father's divine plan of creation? Why was the world created to be his stage? Why was all created for him? Why is he before all else?

Moreover, the second stanza declares that Jesus is likewise the head of the order of redemption: "He is the head of the body, the church; he is the beginning, the first-born from the dead, that in everything he might be pre-eminent [*en pasin autos proteuon* — literally, in all things he holding the first place]" (Col. 1:18). Why is Jesus the head of the body? Why should he be the first to rise in glory and become the Lord of the Church? What has Jesus done that attests to his pre-eminence both in the order of creation and in the order of redemption?

[5] For a discussion of this and other texts concerning the primacy of Christ from a Scotistic perspective, see J.-F. Bonnefoy, *Christ and the Cosmos* (Paterson: St Anthony Guild Press, 1965); M. Meilach, *The Primacy of Christ* (Chicago: Franciscan Herald Press, 1964); Carol, *Why Jesus Christ?*.

[6] The Christology expressed in the colossian Hymn as well as the Christology of John's Prologue grew out of the Wisdom literature of the Old Testament. See Prov 8:22-31; Jb 28; Sir 24; Bar 4; Wis 7:22-30.

For in him all the fullness of God was pleased to dwell, and through him to reconcile to himself all things, whether on earth or in heaven, making peace by the blood of his cross. (Col 1:19-20).

What we should note firstly is that the two orders are embodied and conjoined by one and the same person who is the incarnate Son of God now glorified. All perfection — divine and human — and all actions — divine and human — are predicated on the historical Jesus. Thus the primacy is founded upon what has actually taken place and not on some ahistorical hypothesis.

Secondly, Jesus' pre-eminence is two-fold. He is the eternal Son who shares equally and fully in the Father's divine nature (see Col 2:9). The Father gave to his Son a ranking consistent with who he is. However, Jesus' supremacy is not the result of divine nepotism. Rather, as the obedient son, he reconciles to himself all things. This reconciliation was accomplished at a great price — as one of us, within our sinful condition. While not explicitly stated, we can conclude this because peace is the fruit of the offering of himself on the cross (the mark of sin and condemnation) and the shedding of his holy blood.

Thus, the Colossian hymn testifies to three significant aspects of Jesus' primacy: (1) the primacy of Christ, contrary to gnostic speculation, pertains to the concrete historical Jesus in all his authenticity. It is not concerned with some mythical hero whose valiant deeds are enacted in an imaginary realm; (2) the primacy of Jesus is founded upon the truth that he (this historical man) is Son of God — in him the fullness of divinity dwells bodily; and (3) as man, the Son brought about redemption at the cost of his blood so as to deserve pre-eminence in every way. Accordingly, the primacy of Christ as historically revealed cannot be separated from the condition of sin. Rather, the primacy is actually manifested from within our sinful situation for the sake of our healing. Sin — man's personal sinful condition, the world's sinful history, and especially Jesus' owning of our sinfulness in his humanity — is the milieu from which the supremacy of Christ is established and ratified.

Moreover, the Colossian hymn reminds us that the Christian Church is primarily the gathering of those who have been ransomed from sin, and reconciled to the Father, and have now given their lives to Jesus as their Lord. The Church is that Spirit-filled body of people who acknowledge and live under the headship of Jesus. Christians are precisely those who recognize the primacy of Jesus and profess that they have been created *for Christ.*

The Gospel of John: Behold Your King!

The Gospel of John is an even more articulate witness to the intrinsic relationship between the cross (sin) and Jesus' primacy.[7] John proclaims that we have seen the glory of the only begotten Son (cf. Jn 1:14). The Father sent his Son into the world for our salvation, but inherent in this salvific plan was the Father's desire to reveal the Son's glory (Jn 3:16).

Actually, for John, the salvation of the world is the principal effect of the glorification of the Son. While the glory of Jesus and the salvation of the world are fully achieved and consummated in one and the same act, yet the exaltation of Jesus is logically prior to and the cause of our redemption. Only in

---

[7]Interestingly those historically who argue for the primacy of Christ do not treat the Gospel of John as a whole. This Gospel, of all the New Testament documents, appears to possess, along with the book of Revelation, the most thorough and sustained argument for his primacy. As stated previously, the Gospel of John perceives that what is enacted in time is but the playing out in history of what eternally transpires within the Trinity — the drama of the Father glorifying the Son and the Son in turn glorifying the Father. This mutual glorification is done in and through the reciprocal love of the Holy Spirit.

manifesting the pre-eminent glory of Jesus did the Father bring about the salvation of the world.

Jesus did not seek his own glory, but there is "One who seeks it . . . It is the Father who glorifies me" (Jn 8:50, 54). It was and is the Father's desire that all may honor his Son as they honor him (cf. 5:22-23). The Father redeemed us in Jesus, not for our own sakes, but that we might be the Father's acceptable and holy gift to his Son, for the praise of his Son's glory. Jesus prayed that the Father would glorify him so that those who believe might behold the glory the Father had given him before all time (cf. Jn 17:1, 5, 22): "Father, I desire that they also, whom you have given me, may be with me where I am, to behold my glory which you have given me in your love for me before the foundation of the world" (Jn. 17:24).

Where did the Father most thoroughly manifest the glory of his Son, the glory that he possessed from all eternity? Where did the Father convincingly demonstrate that Jesus is his faithful, obedient, loyal, and loving Son? Where did the Father declare that his Son deserves all glory, praise, and honor — that all primacy is his? It was on the cross.

As we previously described when we studied the passion narrative of John, the cross depicted both Jesus' affinity to our sinful condition and his glory as the only begotten Son. The glory of Jesus resides directly in his willingness to do the Father's will even to dying a sinner's death on the cross. At the moment when Judas left the upper room, in the utter darkness of the world's and history's sin, Jesus proclaimed: "Now is the Son of man glorified, and in him God is glorified; if God is glorified in him, God will also glorify him in himself, and glorify him at once" (Jn. 13:30-32).

Jesus gave glory to his Father through obediently complet-ing his Father's work and, simultaneously, the Father glorified Jesus. The cross, as the mutual giving and receiving of glory between the Father and the Son, was an historical dramatization of the heavenly relationship between the Father and the Son. In the cross, both the Father and Jesus revealed why primacy belongs to Jesus alone — the Father, by allowing the world to see under the most severe conditions of sin how obedient and loving his Son is; and the Son by being obedient and loyal, even within a humanity contaminated by sin and burdened by the condemnation assumed. This is beautifully illustrated in a couple of scenes from the passion narrative.

In the passion narrative, the true nature of Jesus' kingship or primacy is revealed.[8] For John, the trial before Pilate prefigured, anticipated and thus helped interpret the cross. During his interrogation of Jesus, Pilate asked him if he were the King of Jews (cf. Jn 18:33). Jesus answered that his kingship was not of this world (cf. Jn 18:36). At Pilate's insistence that he was nonetheless a king, Jesus responded: 'You say that I am a king. For this I was born, and for this I have come into the world, to bear witness to the truth. Everyone who is of the truth hears my voice" (Jn 18:37-38).

The phrases — "For this I was born, for this I have come into the world" — are purposely equivocal. They indicate that the Son became man in order to be king, and yet, as they are spoken within the context of his trial, they also refer to his imminent passion and death, which is equally the result of his becoming man (sarx). This is exactly what John wishes us to grasp. This is the two-fold truth to which Jesus will soon bear witness and those who are open to the truth will accept in faith. The primacy of Jesus the king is to be manifested on the cross.

An equally revealing scene for John, the central scene of Jesus' trial, takes place at his scourging, for there the soldiers

---

[8]Outside the passion narrative only twice does John's Gospel refer to Jesus' kingship (cf. Jn 6:15; 12:12-15). In both instances, the people desired an earthly ruler.

ironically declare the truth of who Jesus is:[9] "And the soldiers plaited a crown of thorns, and put it on his head, and arrayed him in a purple robe; they came up to him, saying 'Hail, King of the Jews!' and struck him with their hands" (Jn 19:2-3).

Without knowing it, these men proclaimed the truth that would resound both in heaven and on earth. Jesus is the king over all. There is no one greater, not because he conquered by arrogant worldly power, but because he was meek, humble, and rejected. His body, physically now, bore the birthmark of sin, and yet it was this birthmark — the marks of the whip, thorns, nails, and spear — that earned him the crown of glory.

John continues with his progressive typology, that is, using one scene as a type to prefigure, illuminate, and interpret the next. John skilfully composed as parallels the climactic judgment scene before Pilate and the crucifixion. In so doing, he helps the reader perceive the true significance of both. We can see this more easily when we set these texts side by side:

Gabbatha (Jn 19:13-15)	*Golgotha (Jn 19:17-22)*
Pilate… brought Jesus out and sat [him] down on the judgment seat at a place called the Pavement, and in Hebrew, Gabbatha. . . . He said to the Jews, "Behold your King!" They cried out, "Away with him, away with him, crucify him."	Jesus… went out… to the place of a skull, which is called in Hebrew Golgotha. There they crucified himæ… Pilate wrote a title… "Jesus of Nazareth, the King of Jews."… The Jews then said to Pilate: "Do not write…"

The poetic resonance between Gabbatha and Golgotha suggests that John saw a correlation between the events of the

[9]See I. de La Potterie, *The Hour of Jesus*, 75-77.

trial and the crucifixion. Likewise, Jesus' movement helps to establish the parallelism. He moved from inside the Praetorium to the court scene outside; he moved from inside Jerusalem to Calvary outside the city. More importantly, what did John wish us to see through our eyes of faith?[10]

At Gabbatha, Pilate sat Jesus upon the imperial seat of judgment, and in so doing ironically declared that the one who is being judged is the true judge.[11] He likewise prophetically proclaimed Jesus, a man despised and detested, to be king. On the cross, this prophecy was fulfilled. Jesus, "a man of sorrows, and acquainted with grief," one stricken, smitten, and afflicted with sin, triumphed over sin, Satan, and death (see Is 53:3-4). For John, the cross was the consummate sign of contradiction. The cross — loathsome and revolting — was Jesus' throne of glory because, in and through his most abject lowliness and humility — the burden of our sin — he manifested his absolute faithfulness to the Father and his unconditional and all-consuming love for us. The cross affirmed the primacy of Christ, the fullness of his glory.

Again ironically, Pilate wrote in three languages for all the world to read the Father's verdict and nailed it on the cross: "Jesus of Nazareth, the King of the Jews" (Jn 19:19). This man Jesus, suspended upon the cross, is King and Lord. In him, the fullness of glory dwells and to him belong all praise and honor. When challenged (by the people then and now), Pilate echoed the eternal words of the Father: "What I have written I have written" (Jn. 19:22). The cross is the Father's final, definitive, and unalterable decree of Jesus' primacy.[12]

---

[10]See *ibid.*, 90-95.

[11]There is some discussion as to who sat down on the seat of judgment — Pilate or Jesus. See *ibid.*, pp. 82-86.

[12]The Acts of the Apostles testifies to this same truth. The one whom the people denied and delivered up, the one rejected and scorned, is the very

As we noted in the Colossian hymn, so too in John's Gospel: the Church is composed of those who recognize the truth that their King is the crucified Jesus. Mary and John, standing beneath the cross and gazing up in faith, having been washed clean in his blood and reborn in the water of the Spirit, represent and prefigure the Church of all time (cf. Jn 19:25-27, 31-37). Even doubting Thomas became the epitome of a man of faith. By placing his fingers into the nail marks in Jesus' hands and his hand into his side, he is the first to proclaim publicly that the one who took upon himself our sin (manifested in the now glorious wounds) is "My Lord and My God" (Jn 20:28). These two scenes illustrate as well that salvation is but the primary effect of Jesus' own prior glorification.

The Book of Revelation: Worthy is the Lamb Who was Slain

The book of Revelation anticipates the heavenly worship where the glory of Christ's primacy will be revealed in full.[13] Yet even in heaven, the Lord of lords and the King of kings, the Alpha and the Omega, the First and the Last still bears the brandmarks of sin now made radiant — "He is clad in a robe dipped in blood" (Rev 19:13). For it is the Lamb who was slain who is honored and glorified and he alone is exalted and praised expressly because he bore our sin and died on our behalf (cf. Rev 5:6):

---

one whom the Father has raised up and glorified. He would not let his holy one see corruption (see Ps 16:10). "Let all the house of Israel therefore know assuredly that God has made him both Lord and Christ, this Jesus whom you crucified" (Acts 2:36, cf. Acts 2:22-36; 3:12-16; 4:8-12). The Letter to the Hebrews similarly states: "When he had made purification for sin, he sat down at the right hand of the Majesty on high, having become as much superior to angels as the name he has obtained is more excellent than theirs" (Heb 1:3-4).

[13]For the literary and theological background to the book of Revelation, see Adela Yarbro Collins, *The New Jerome Biblical Commentary*, 996-1000.

> Worthy are you to take the scroll and to open its seals, for
> you were slain and by your blood did ransom men for God
> from every tribe and tongue and people and nation, and has
> made them a kingdom and priests to our God, and they shall
> reign on earth. (Rev 5:9-10).

> Worthy is the Lamb who was slain, to receive power, and
> wealth and wisdom and might and honor and glory and
> blessing! . . . To him who sits upon the throne and to the
> Lamb be blessing and honor and glory and might for ever
> and ever! (Rev 5:12-13).

Multitudes in white robes washed clean in the blood of the Lamb
— the heavenly church, "the wife of the Lamb" — acclaim their
crucified Lord: "Salvation belongs to our God who sits upon the
throne and to the Lamb!" (Rev 21:9; 7:10, cf. 7:14; 12:11; 19:6-
9). The glory of the cross, the lamp of the Lamb, eternally
illumines the whole of heaven (see Rev 21:22-23).

We need to examine one final controverted passage. Revelation 13:8 is variously translated: "And all who dwell on earth
will worship it [the beast], every one whose name has not been
written before the foundation of the world in the book of life
of the Lamb that was slain" (cf. RSV, NRSV, NJB, NAB). Or:
"All the inhabitants of the earth will worship it [the beast], all
whose names have not been written in the book of life of the
Lamb, slain since the foundation of the world" (cf. REB, NIV,
NRSV as alternative translation). What was from the foundation of the world — the names written in the book of life, or
the Lamb that was slain?

The structure of the Greek text is such that it would seem
that "from the foundation of the world" (*apo kataboles kosmou*)
modifies the Lamb who was slain and not the names written in
the book of life. The reason the majority of contemporary

English versions do not prefer this translation seems to be two-fold. Revelation 17:8 expressly states that the names of those who will be saved were written in the book of life from the foundation of the world, so confirming Revelation 13:8. Also this translation seems to make more sense since Jesus was slain in time and history and not from the foundation of the world.[14]

However, within the eternal plan of God, it is only because the Lamb, burdened with our sin, was slain that he conquered all his enemies (the beast), procured his throne, and secured those whose names are written in his book of life. In other words, the Father, from before the world began, predicated and pre-ordained the primacy of Christ the Lamb, totally and exclusively, on the cross. Within the Father's mind, the cross is not an afterthought to the glorification of his Son, but rather the pre-eminent demonstration and actual attainment of Jesus' primacy. The First Letter to Peter confirms this judgment:

> You know that you were ransomed from the futile ways inherited from your fathers, not with perishable things such as silver or gold, but with the precious blood of Christ, like that of a lamb without blemish or spot. He was destined before the foundation of the world but was made manifest at the end of the times for your sake. Through him you have confidence in God, who raised him from the dead and gave him glory, so that your faith and hope are in God. (1 Pt 1:18-21).

Manifestly, even from our brief study, the salvific reasons for the Incarnation converge with and enhance the truth of Jesus'

---

[14]Cf. G. R. Beasley-Murray, *The Book of Revelation* (The New Century Bible) (Greenwood, S.C.: Attic Press, 1978), 213-214.

primacy. Our approach has been wholly biblical and historical, and thus in keeping with Aquinas' concerns, and yet has upheld Scotus' insight that the supremacy of Jesus was first in the Father's mind. These valid convictions of Aquinas and Scotus form parts of a deeper and more central truth. The primacy of the Incarnate Son is manifested in his taking on our sinful flesh and in his redemptive death on the cross. Jesus showed forth his eternal glory in reconciling the world to God.

CONCLUSION: IN NO OTHER NAME

This study has attempted to establish and demonstrate the importance of Jesus' fallen human condition. When the eternal Son of the Father entered into our world, under the then-present conditions, he came to exist as man touched and altered by the reality of sin. He was a son of Adam. He assumed our sinful flesh.

Within this humanity, the Son lived an obedient life under the guidance and power of the Holy Spirit, fending off all temptation, and thus fulfilling all righteousness. His righteous, loving obedience culminated on the cross where, through the offering of his holy and innocent life, he both reconciled us to the Father and put our sinful nature to death. So pleased was the Father that he raised his Son to glory, giving him a complete and incorruptible humanity.

Through conversion, faith, and baptism, we experience what happened to Jesus. our sinful flesh shares in the death of Jesus and we participate in his new humanity. By the Spirit, we come to live in Christ, the new Adam. By coming to live in Christ, we become sons and daughters of the Father. We become members of the Church, brothers and sisters in Christ's body. We take on the holiness of God, becoming temples of the Holy Spirit. We are thus transfigured into the very likeness of Christ, anticipating the fullness of glory in heaven. We look now for that promised us when the inheritance will be ours.

This study advances the cause of many contemporary christological concerns, which are a work of the Spirit in our day in the following ways:

1. By accentuating the fallen humanity of Jesus, the Incarnation captures a fresh authenticity. The eternal Son does truly know our human condition, in all its frailty. He can identify with all our human adversity and affliction — the mystery of evil in all its forms.

   Moreover, by granting Jesus' earthly humanity its proper condition, we have also confirmed the intrinsic affinity between God's activity in the Old Testament and in the New. As God humbled himself (*kenosis*) to come among the unrighteous in the past, so now by assuming our sinful flesh, Jesus is truly Emmanuel — God among us;

2. In the past, many have lamented the divorce between classical Christology and soteriology. The Incarnation rarely inspired a theology of the cross and resurrection. This study, again by illuminating the significance of Jesus' fallen condition, demonstrates how closely related, by necessity, are the Incarnation and the cross. What is not assumed is not saved;

3. We hear similar laments that classical Christology has no place for Pneumatology. The humanity of Jesus ran on the steam of the divinity. However, by acknowledging the human limitations of Jesus due to sin, the Spirit assumes his appropriate and proper function. Jesus lived and died in the Spirit. Only through the Spirit could he defend himself against temptation and only in the Spirit could he remain faithful to the Spirit's anointing, that of being the Servant/Son. In the Spirit, too, he offered his human life to the Father on the cross. In turn, the Spirit transfigured Jesus' lowly body into his glorious humanity;

4. We have emphasized the personal human actions of Jesus. He accomplished his work in a responsible, human manner. His obedience was a dynamic laying hold of his Father's will

so much so that obedience defined and revealed the essence of his Sonship.

Moreover, the love for the Father bore the strength of genuine suffering. The cross testifies to this truth. There Jesus, with his whole human heart and will, gave his life to the Father. There he resolutely put sin to death. The cross shows the fiber of the man;

5. As point number 3 and 4 exemplify, this study not only gives proper scope to the Holy Spirit, but also, by allowing the humanity of Jesus to assume its proper theological rank, enhances the place of the Father within Christology. As man, under our fallen conditions, Jesus was called to revere and obey the Father as an only Son. It was the Father's plan that he fulfilled as one of us on our behalf;

6. Moreover, this essay has stressed through free, Spirit-empowered human action, Jesus substantially changed reality. What was not possible before is now possible. This is clear throughout the New Testament documents. Our relationship with God and with others can be on a completely new and different level. We are transformed. The changes that Jesus' human actions have attained differ in kind from the accomplishments of anyone else. This is the reason contemporary men and women should reverence Jesus in gratitude;

7. Likewise, the redemption and transformation of Jesus' humanity have given new realism to our eschatological hope. As Jesus was freed from the corruption of sin and death and now reigns as a glorified man, so too are we called to share in this same promise. We long for the new heaven and the new earth where the tears of sin and death will be wiped away so we can live in the presence of the all-consuming God;

8. In giving due theological depth to the humanity of Jesus, we have hopefully given greater insight as well into an authentic Christology "from below". Only in and through this hu-

manity, corrupted by sin, did the Son of God reveal his genuine and absolute divinity and win for us our salvation. Thus, we have also grounded a Christology "from above", i.e., that it was truly the Son of God who came to exist as man; and

9. Lastly, we can now clearly identify the absolute definitiveness of Jesus. Because of who he is as the Son of God incarnate and because of what he has done as man, he is preeminent in every way. The primacy belongs to him alone, for there obviously "is salvation in no one else, for there is no other name under heaven given among men by which we must be saved" (Acts 4:12).

AUTHOR'S POSTSCRIPT:
THE IMMACULATE CONCEPTION AND THE SINFUL HUMANITY OF JESUS

In his kind Foreword to this work Dr Gunton raised the issue of the Mary's Immaculate Conception in light of the "sinful humanity" of Jesus. While I was not unaware of this question, I had felt that it better to address the strictly christological issues involved in my thesis — that Jesus possessed a humanity of the sinful race of Adam — and not take up this more mariological issue. However, in light of Dr Gunton's question, I now see more clearly that the Roman Catholic doctrine of Mary's Immaculate Conception bears more on this Christological concern than I may had first recognized. This is especially so if the Immaculate Conception is perceived as a stumbling block to the acceptance of my thesis or that my thesis is construed as undermining or jeopardizing Mary's sinlessness. I would neither want Catholics to lessen their faith in the Immaculate Conception because of the arguments I have put forth here concerning Jesus' humanity, nor would I want what I have said about Jesus to hinder Protestants from accepting the Immaculate Conception. Therefore with Dr Gunton's kind allowance, I thought it wise to add a short postscript on the relationship between the Immaculate Conception and Jesus' "sinful humanity".

Dr Gunton believes that my thesis, that in the Incarnation the eternal Son of God assumed a humanity of the sinful race of Adam, is logically incompatible with the Catholic doctrine of the Immaculate Conception. The logic would presumably run something like this: If Jesus' humanity bore the birth-mark of sin, as I have argued, then Mary could not be sinless herself for she is his mother and thus the source of his sin marred human nature. Vice-versa, if Mary is sinless, then Jesus would not have a humanity of the sinful race of Adam, but would have assumed an "immaculate" humanity like her own. To answer this seemingly theological conundrum it is necessary to discern exactly what the Catholic Church holds when it proclaims that Mary was immaculately conceived.

I cannot, nor am I competent, to take up now the whole historical development of the doctrine of the Immaculate Conception. I wish only briefly to comment on the Bull *Ineffabilis Deus* of Pope Pius IX given on December 8, 1854 in which he infallibly defined Mary's Immaculate Conception. The relevant passage reads:

> We declare, pronounce and define: the doctrine that maintains that the most Blessed Virgin Mary in the first instant of her conception, by a unique grace and privilege of the omnipotent God and in consideration of the merits of Christ Jesus the Savior of the human race, was preserved free from all stain of original sin, is a doctrine revealed by God and therefore must be firmly and constantly held by all the faithful (Denz. 2803).

A number of points must be made. Firstly, the preservation of Mary from all stain of original sin is predicated upon and in anticipation of "the merits of Jesus Christ the Savior of the human race". Mary did not merit this singular grace. God freely bestowed it upon her in light of the salvific work of his Son, Jesus. Jesus won this grace for Mary, as a member of the human race, through his own death to sin and new life with God.

Secondly, the crucial issue is: What does it mean to say that Mary "was preserved free from all stain of original sin?" I would argue that the Catholic Church is proclaiming that Mary was preserved from all *moral* stain of original sin. Never was she separated from God. She possessed from the moment of conception the justifying and sanctifying life in the Holy Spirit, and thus never personally bore the guilt and condemnation of Adam's sin. She was also preserved from all concupiscence — our normal interior propensity to sin. From the moment of her conception she was made holy by the indwelling Spirit and so interiorly preserved from all stain of sin.

If my interpretation of the doctrine of the Immaculate Conception is correct, I would proceed to argue that this doctrine does not mean that Mary was preserved from all the exterior effects of original sin, those that do not touch her subjective moral and spiritual rectitude. While she was like her son in that he also was holy from conception and freed from concupiscence (the fomes of sin), she was also like her son in that she too inherited a humanity of Adam's race and so experienced the effects of our fallen world.

Thus Mary experienced temptation, not as something arising from within her, but as coming from without which she, like Jesus, had continually to stand firmly against. She too bore the attacks of Satan. And as I argued concerning Jesus, Mary's experience of temptations and satanic assaults, far from being less severe than ours, were intensified precisely because they confronted her undivided holiness which demanded that she not entertain them in the slightest manner. Likewise, she could also suffer — physically and emotionally. Moreover, her humanity was still under the sentence of death and so she too must die (as did Jesus) and come to share fully in the resurrection of her son. (While some theologians in the past have held that Mary did not die, the stronger tradition — in both the East and West — is that she did die and did so precisely because, that while she was sinless, she still possessed a humanity of the race of Adam. It was only after she died that she was assumed bodily into heaven.) To say that Mary is immaculate is not to say that she lived a charmed life, that God placed her in a spiritual Disneyland where nothing of sin and evil touched her. Second only to her son, Mary experienced and knew the full and complete horror of sin and evil. She too longed to be set free from this body and world of death so as to live fully with God.

I believe that a study of the New Testament, one that I cannot carry out here, would confirm this assessment of Mary's life. We only need to consider Simeon's prophesy that a sword would pierce her heart (cf. Lk. 2:34-35), the flight into Egypt(Mth. 2:13-15), and above all her place beneath the cross of her son in order to recognize that Mary must have experienced the full weight of sin and evil, anguishing in soul and body, and yet standing firm in faith before God.

It is evident then that I do not see that my thesis that Jesus' possessed a humanity of the fallen race of Adam is in any way incompatible with the doctrine of the Immaculate Conception. What I have said of Jesus' humanity can equally be said of Mary's, except that her sinless humanity was the fruit of her son's death and resurrection. While Mary was preserved from the moral corruption of sin with its crippling spiritual aftermath, yet it was from her that Jesus, in direct line with Adam, inherited a humanity marred and disfigured by sin.

Dr Gunton said that he did not want to tempt me "into indiscretion". By provoking me to take up the question of the doctrine of the Immaculate Conception and the "sinful humanity" of Jesus I do not think that he has, at least I hope that he has not. Instead he may have given me the opportunity to speak of both in a manner that would contribute to the growth of a common faith between Catholics and Protestants. To have done this is a true work of the Spirit on Dr Gunton's part.

SELECT BIBLIOGRAPHY

Aldwinckle, R. F., *More Than Man: A Study in Christology*. Grand Rapids: Eerdmans, 1976.

Alfaro, J., Grillmeier, A., Schulte, R., Schutz, Ch., Widerkehr, D., *Mysterium Salutis* 11 *Christologie et Vie du Christ*. Paris: Les Editions du Cerf, 1975.

Anderson, R. S., *Historical Transcendence and the Reality of God: A Christological Critique*. London: Geoffrey Chapman, 1976.

Anselm, *St Anselm: Basic Writings*, trs. S. N. Deane. La Salle: Open Court Press, 1968.

Barth, K., *Church Dogmatics*, trs. G. T. Thomson and H. Knight. Edinburgh: T. & T. Clark, 1956.

Beare, F. W., *The Gospel According to Matthew*. San Francisco: Harper and Row, 1981.

Beasley-Murray, G. R., *The Book of Revelation*. Greenwood, SC: Attic Press, 1978.

Bernard of Clairvaux. *On the Song of Songs*, trs. K. Walsh. Kalamazoo, MI: Cistercian Publications, 1981.

Bettenson, H., *The Early Christian Fathers*. Oxford: University Press, 1956.

The Latter Christian Fathers. Oxford: University Press, 1970.

Bloesch, D., "Process Theology in Reformed Perspective," *Listening* 14 (1979) 185-195.

Bonnefoy, J.-F., *Christ and Cosmos*. Paterson: St Anthony Guild Press, 1965.

Branick, V., "The Sinful Flesh of the Son of God (Rom 8:3): A Key Image of Pauline Theology," *The Catholic Biblical Quarterly* 47 (1985) 246-262.

Brown, R., *Biblical Reflections on Crises Facing the Church*. New York: Paulist Press, 1975.

The Gospel According to John (The Anchor Bible). New York: Doubleday, 1966.

The Birth of the Messiah. Garden City: Doubleday, 1977.

Brown, R., Fitzmyer, J., Murphy, R. E., eds., *The New Jerome Biblical Commentary*. Englewood Cliffs: Prentice Hall, 1990.

Bruce, A. B., *The Humiliation of Christ*. Edinburgh: T. & T. Clark, 1881.

Bruce, F. F., *Commentary on Galatians* (NIGTC). Grand Rapids: Eerdmans, 1982.

Callahan, A., *Karl Rahner's Spirituality of the Pierced Heart: A Reinterpration of Devotion to the Sacred Heart*. Washington, DC: University Press of America, 1990.

Carol, J., *Why Jesus Christ: Thomistic, Scotistic and Conciliatory Perspectives*. Manassas, VI: Trinity Communications, 1986.

Cranfield, C. E. B., *The Epistle to the Romans*. Edinburgh; T. & T. Clark, 1975.

Cullman, O., *The Christology of the New Testament*. Philadelphia: Westminster Press, 1959.

de la Potterie, I., *The Hour of Jesus*. New York: Alba House, 1989.

Dodd, C. H., *The Epistle of Paul to the Romans* (MNTC). New York: Harper and Row, 1959.

Dunn, J. D. G., *Christology in the Making*. Philadelphia: Westminster Press, 1980.

Fitzmyer, J., *The Gospel According to Luke*, (The Anchor Bible). New York: Doubleday, 1981.

Fuller, R., *The Foundations of New Testament Christology*. London: Collins, 1965.

Fuller, R. and Perkins, P., *Who Is This Christ?* Philadelphia: Westminster Press, 1983.

Galot, J., *La Conscience de Jesus*. Gembloux: Duculot-Lethielleux, 1977.

Who Is Christ? Chicago: Franciscan Herald Press, 1981.

The Person of Christ. Chicago: Franciscan Herald Press, 1983.

Gore, C., *The Incarnation of the Son of God: The Bampton Lectures 1891.* London: John Murray, 1898.

Griffin, D., *A Process Christology.* Philadelphia; Westminster Press, 1973.

Grillmeier, A., *Christ in Christian Tradition.* Vol. 1. Atlanta: John Knox Press, 1975.

Gunton, C., "Two Dogmas Revisited: Edward Irving's Christology," *The Scottish Journal of Theology* 41 (1988) 366ff.

Hall, J., *The Kenotic Theory.* New York: Longmans, Green and Co., 1898.

Henry, P., "Kenose," *Dictionnaire de la Bible Supplement,* Vol. 5. Paris: 1957.

Hellwig, M., *Jesus, the Compassion of God.* Wilmington, DE: Michael Glazier, 1983.

"Re-Emergence of the Human, Critical, Public Jesus," *Theological Studies* 50 (1989) 466-480.

Herve, J. M., *Manuale Theologiae Dogmaticae.* paris: Apud Berche et Pagis, 1959.

Hick, J., ed., *The Myth of God Incarnate.* London: SCM, 1977.

Hopkins, J., *A Companion to the Study of St Anselm.* Minneapolis: University of Minnesota Press, 1972.

Hopkins, J. and Richardson, H., eds., *Anselm of Canterbury: Trinity, Incarnation, and Redemption.* New York: Harper Torch Books, 1970.

Hughes, P. E., *A Commentary on the Epistle to the Hebrews.* Grand Rapids: Eerdmans, 1977.

Irving, E., *The Collected Writings of Edward Irving in Five Volumes,* ed. G. Carlyle. London: Alexander Strachan, 1865.

Jeremias, J., *The Prayers of Jesus.* STB II 6 London: 1967.
New Testament Theology, I. London: SCM, 1972.

Johnson, E., *Consider Jesus: Waves of Renewal in Christology.* New York: Crossroad, 1990.

Kehl, M. and Loser, W., eds., Daly, R. and Lawrence, F., trs. *The Von Balthasar Reader.* New York: Crossroad: 1982.

Kelly, J. N. D., *Early Christian Doctrines.* London: Adam & Charles Black, 1968.

Kittle, G., Friedrich, G., eds., *Theological Dictionary of the New Testament.* Grand Rapids; Eerdmans, 1971.

Knox, J., *The Humanity and Divinity of Christ.* Cambridge: University Press, 1967.

Kung, H., *On Being A Christian.* Garden City, NY: Doubleday, 1967.

Krasevac, E., "'Christology From Above' And 'Christology From Below'", *The Thomist* 51 (1987) 299-306.

Kummel, W. G., *The Theology of the New Testament.* Nashville: Abingdon Press, 1978.

Laurentin, R., *The Truth of Christmas.* Petersham, MA: St Bede's Publications, 1986.

Lawton, J. S., *Conflict in Christology.* London: SPCK, 1947.

Lonergan, B., *Collection,* ed. F. Crowe. New York: Herder and Herder, 1967.

Lyonnet, S., *Exegesis Epistulae Ad Romanos.* Romae: Pontificium Institutum Biblicum, 1962.

MacGregor, G., *He Who Lets Us Be: A Theology of Love.* New York: Seabury, 1975.

McIntyre, J., *St Anselm and His Critics.* London: 1954.

Marshall, I. H., *I Believe in the Historical Jesus.* Grand Rapids: Eerdmans, 1977.

   The Origins of New Testament Christology. Downers Grove, IL: InterVaristy Press, 1976.

   Jesus the Savior: Studies in the New Testament. Downers Grove, IL: InterVarsity Press, 1990.

Martin, F., "Historical Criticism and New Testament Teaching on Imitation of Christ," *Anthropotes* 6 (1990) 261-287.

Meilach, M., *The Primacy of Christ.* Chicago: Franciscan Herald Press, 1964.

Meyendorff, J., *Christ in Eastern Christian Thought.* New York: St Vladimir's Press, 1975.

   Byzantine Theology. New York: Fordham University Press, 1979.

Morris, T. V., *The Logic of God Incarnate.* Ithaca: Cornell University Press, 1986.

Moule, C. F. D., *The Origin of Christology.* Cambridge: University Press, 1977.

Newman, J. H., *An Essay on the Development of Christian Doctrine.* Garden City, NY: Image Books, 1960.
Parochial and Plain Sermons. San Francisco: Ignatius Press, 1987.

O'Collins, G., *What are They Saying About Jesus?* New York: Paulist Press, 1977.
Interpreting Jesus. New York: Paulist Press, 1983.
O'Donnell, J., *The Mystery of the Triune God.* New York: Paulist Press, 1990.

Pelikan, J., *Jesus Through the Centuries: His Place in the History of Culture.* New York: Harper and Row, 1985.
Pittenger, N., *Process Thought and Christian Faith.* New York: Macmillan, 1968.
Christology Reconsidered. London: SCM, 1970.
Potvin, T. R., *The Theology of the Primacy of Christ According to St Thomas and it Scriptural Foundations,* (Studia Friburgensia; New Series, 50). Fribourg, Switzerland: University Press, 1973.
Prestige, G. L., *God in Patristic Thought.* London: SPCK, 1952.

Rahner, K., *Theological Investigations,* Vol. 1. Baltimore: Helicon Press, 1961.
Theological Investigations, Vol. 3. Baltimore: Helicon Press, 1967.
Theological Investigations, Vol. 7. New York: Herder and Herder, 1971.
Ratzinger, J., "Zum Personenverstandnis in der Theologie," *Dogma und Verkundingung.* Munich: Erich Wewel Verlag, 1973. English translation, "Concerning the Notion of Person in Theology," *Communio* 17 (Fall 1990) 439-454.
Richard, L. J., *A Kenotic Christology.* Washington, DC: University Press of America, 1982.
Robinson, J. A. T., *The Human Face of God.* London: SCM, 1973.

Sanders, E. P., *Jesus and Judaism.* Philadelphia: Fortress Press, 1985.
Schaff, P., ed., *Nicene and Post-Nicene Fathers.* Grand Rapids: Eerdmans, 1978 repr.
Schillebeeckx, E., *Jesus: An Experiment in Christology.* New York: Seabury Press, 1979.
Sellers, R. V., *The Council of Chalcedon.* London: SPCK, 1961.

Senior, D., *Jesus, A Gospel Portrait.* Dayton: Pflaum Press, 1975.

Sloyan, G., *Jesus in Focus: A Life in Its Setting.* Mystic, CT: Twenty-Third Publications, 1983.

Strachan, G., *The Pentecostal Theology of Edward Irving.* Peabody, MA: Hendrickson Publishers, 1973.

Sturch, R., *The Word and the Christ.* Oxford: Clarendon Press, 1991.

Tambasco, A., *In the Days of Jesus: the Jewish Background and Unique Teaching of Jesus.* New York: Paulist Press, 1983.

Thomas Aquinas, *Summa Theologica,* trs. Dominican Fathers. New York: Benzinger Brothers, 1947.
    Summa Contra Gentiles, trs. *On the Truth of the Catholic Faith,* eds. H. Anderson, A. Pegis, V. J. Bourke, and J. O'Neil. (Garden City: Image Books, 1955-1957.)

Vanhoye, A., *Old Testament Priests and the New Priest.* Petersham, MA: St Bede's Publications, 1986.

Vermes, G., *Jesus the Jew.* Philadelphia: Fortress Press, 1981.

von Balthasar, Hans Urs, *Mysterium Paschale,* trs. A. Nichols. Edinburgh: T. & T. Clark, 1990.

Wainwright, G., *Doxology.* Oxford: University Press, 1980.

Weinandy, T., *Does God Change?: The Word's Becoming in the Incarnation.* Petersham, MA: St Bede's Press, 1985.

Weston, F., *The One Christ.* London: Longmans, Green, and Co., 1914.

INDEX OF NAMES

Hippolytus, 17.
Honorius I, 36-37.
Hopkins, J., 40, 44.
Hughes, P.E., 121.

Ignatius of Antioch, 25.
Irenaeus, 26-28.
Irving, E., x, 54, 56-61, 64.

Jeremias, J., 5.
John Chrysostom, 51.
John Paul II, 56.
Johnson, E., 3, 5.
Julian of Halicanassus, 35.

Karris, R.J., 104, 129.
Kelly, J.N.D., 17.
Kittle, G., 76.
Knox, J., 4.
Krasevac, E., 16.
Kummel, W.G., 76-77.
Kung, H., 16.

Lawton, J.S., 8.
Leo the Great, 35-36.
Leontius of Byzantium, 35.
Lepicier, A., 52.
Lombard, P., 135.
Lonergan, B., 13, 52.
Luther, M., 64.

MacGregor, G., 8.
McIntyre, J., 40.
Macquarrie, J., 4
Marshall, I.H., 6, 96, 114, 126, 127.
Martin, F., 14.

Meilach, M., 138.
Meier, J., 114.
Menken, G., 61.
Meyendorff, J., 35.
Moloney, F., 114.
Morris, T.V., 8, 18.
Moule, C.F.D., 6, 126.
Murphy, R.E., 74.

Nestorius, 10, 33.
Newman, J.H., 21, 64-65.

O'Collins, G., 4, 6, 127.
O'Donnell, J., 12, 69.
Oecolampadius, 64.
Origen, 17, 26.
Owen, J., x.

Patvin, T.R., 136.
Pelikan, J., 113.
Perkins, P., 5.
Pittenger, N., 4, 87.
Pius IX, 154.
Pius XII, 4.
Prestige, G.L., 12.

Rahner, K., 4, 92.
Ratzinger, J., 12.
Richard, L., 8.
Richardson, H., 44.
Robinson, J.A.T., 4.

Sanders, E.P., 5.
Schleiermacher, F.D.E., 55.
Schillebeeckx, E., 14.
Schulte, R., 79, 92.
Schulz, E., 93, 95, 102.

INDEX OF SUBJECTS

INDEX OF KEY NEW TESTAMENT
SCRIPTURES